Praise for *Nellie McClung*

"Both McClung and Gray have set the bar high for women and writers alike, and this is an inspired pairing of tale and teller." —*The Globe and Mail*

"Gray's persistent research means we have a detailed portrait of the times and the issues, and a very lively read." —*National Post*

"With her talent for making history spring to life, Charlotte Gray fills her lively account of McClung's life with wit, political perspective and well-observed detail ... Compulsively readable." —*London Free Press*

"Compelling." —*Canada's History* magazine

Praise for the Extraordinary Canadians series

"These books are not definitive biography; rather, they are opportunities to deepen the relationship between Canadians of the past and Canadians of the present. May this dialogue continue, so that today's biographers themselves will be the subject of the next wave of writers." —*The Globe and Mail*

"Entertaining, literary and informative."   *—National Post*

"Excellent."   *—Winnipeg Free Press*

"The concept of the series is a good one, especially the emphasis on brevity."   *—The Walrus*

"Don't be put off by the charming simplicity of format and language of these books. There's a depth and passion to them that is compelling."   *—Canada's History* magazine

"A series to collect and cherish. As ambitious a publishing program as has been seen in years, it is a reminder of how good a biography can be." *—The SunTimes* (Owen Sound)

PENGUIN CANADA

NELLIE McCLUNG

CHARLOTTE GRAY is one of Canada's best-known writers and biographers, and the award-winning author of several bestsellers, including *Gold Diggers: Striking It Rich on the Klondike*, *Reluctant Genius: The Passions and Inventions of Alexander Graham Bell*, *Mrs. King: The Life and Times of Isabel Mackenzie King*, and *Sisters in the Wilderness: The Lives of Susanna Moodie and Catharine Parr Traill*. An adjunct research professor in the department of history at Carleton University, Gray chairs the board of Canada's National History Society. Charlotte and her husband live in Ottawa.

Nellie McClung

by CHARLOTTE GRAY

With an Introduction by
John Ralston Saul
SERIES EDITOR

EXTRAORDINARY
CANADIANS

PENGUIN CANADA

Published by the Penguin Group

Penguin Group (Canada), 90 Eglinton Avenue East, Suite 700, Toronto, Ontario, Canada M4P 2Y3
(a division of Pearson Canada Inc.)

Penguin Group (USA) Inc., 375 Hudson Street, New York, New York 10014, U.S.A.
Penguin Books Ltd, 80 Strand, London WC2R 0RL, England
Penguin Ireland, 25 St Stephen's Green, Dublin 2, Ireland (a division of Penguin Books Ltd)
Penguin Group (Australia), 250 Camberwell Road, Camberwell, Victoria 3124, Australia
(a division of Pearson Australia Group Pty Ltd)
Penguin Books India Pvt Ltd, 11 Community Centre, Panchsheel Park, New Delhi – 110 017, India
Penguin Group (NZ), 67 Apollo Drive, Rosedale, Auckland 0632, New Zealand
(a division of Pearson New Zealand Ltd)
Penguin Books (South Africa) (Pty) Ltd, 24 Sturdee Avenue, Rosebank,
Johannesburg 2196, South Africa

Penguin Books Ltd, Registered Offices: 80 Strand, London WC2R 0RL, England

First published in Penguin Canada hardcover by Penguin Group (Canada),
a division of Pearson Canada Inc., 2008

Published in this edition, 2011

1 2 3 4 5 6 7 8 9 10 (WEB)

Copyright © Charlotte Gray, 2008
Introduction copyright © John Ralston Saul, 2008

Manufactured in Canada.

LIBRARY AND ARCHIVES CANADA CATALOGUING IN PUBLICATION

Gray, Charlotte, 1948–
Nellie McClung / by Charlotte Gray ; with an introduction by John Ralston Saul.

(Extraordinary Canadians)
Includes bibliographical references.
ISBN 978-0-14-305455-9

1. McClung, Nellie L., 1873–1951. 2. Feminists—Canada—Biography.
3. Authors, Canadian (English)—20th century—Biography. I. Title.
II. Series: Extraordinary Canadians

HQ1455.M3G73 2011   305.42092   C2011-902528-0

Visit the Penguin Group (Canada) website at www.penguin.ca

Special and corporate bulk purchase rates available; please see
www.penguin.ca/corporatesales or call 1-800-810-3104, ext. 2477 or 2474

I HAVE SEEN MY COUNTRY EMERGE from obscurity into one of the truly great nations of the world. I have seen strange things come to pass in the short span of one lifetime, and I hasten to set it down while the light holds. People must know the past to understand the present and to face the future. . . .

In Canada we are developing a pattern of life and I know something about one block of that pattern. I know it for I helped to make it, and I can say that now without any pretense of modesty, or danger of arrogance, for I know that we who make the patterns are not important, but the pattern is.

Nellie L. McClung
THE STREAM RUNS FAST

CONTENTS

INTRODUCTION BY

John Ralston Saul

How do civilizations imagine themselves? One way is for each of us to look at ourselves through our society's most remarkable figures. I'm not talking about hero worship or political iconography. That is a danger to be avoided at all costs. And yet people in every country do keep on going back to the most important people in their past.

This series of Extraordinary Canadians brings together rebels, reformers, martyrs, writers, painters, thinkers, political leaders. Why? What is it that makes them relevant to us so long after their deaths?

For one thing, their contributions are there before us, like the building blocks of our society. More important than that are their convictions and drive, their sense of what is right and wrong, their willingness to risk all, whether it be their lives, their reputations, or simply being wrong in public. Their ideas, their triumphs and failures, all of these somehow constitute a mirror of our society. We look at these people, all dead, and discover what we have been, but also what we can be. A mirror is an instrument for measuring ourselves. What we see can be both a warning and an encouragement.

These eighteen biographies of twenty key Canadians are centred on the meaning of each of their lives. Each of them is very different, but these are not randomly chosen great figures. Together they produce a grand sweep of the creation of modern Canada, from our first steps as a democracy in 1848 to our questioning of modernity late in the twentieth century.

All of them except one were highly visible on the cutting edge of their day while still in their twenties, thirties, and forties. They were young, driven, curious. An astonishing level of fresh energy surrounded them and still does. We in the twenty-first century talk endlessly of youth, but power today is often controlled by people who fear the sort of risks and innovations embraced by everyone in this series. A number of them were dead—hanged, infected on a battlefield, broken by their exertions—well before middle age. Others hung on into old age, often profoundly dissatisfied with themselves.

Each one of these people has changed you. In some cases you know this already. In others you will discover how through these portraits. They changed the way the world hears music, thinks of war, communicates. They changed how each of us sees what surrounds us, how minorities are treated, how we think of immigrants, how we look after each other, how we imagine ourselves through what are now our stories.

You will notice that many of them were people of the word. Not just the writers. Why? Because civilizations are built around many themes, but they require a shared public language. So Laurier, Bethune, Douglas, Riel, LaFontaine, McClung, Trudeau, Lévesque, Big Bear, even Carr and Gould, were masters of the power of language. Beaverbrook was one of the most powerful newspaper publishers of his day. Countries need action and laws and courage. But civilization is not a collection of prime ministers. Words, words, words—it is around these that civilizations create and imagine themselves.

The authors I have chosen for each subject are not the obvious experts. They are imaginative, questioning minds from among our leading writers and activists. They have, each one of them, a powerful connection to their subject. And in their own lives, each is engaged in building what Canada is now becoming.

That is why a documentary is being filmed around each subject. Images are yet another way to get at each subject and to understand their effect on us.

There has not been a biographical project as ambitious as this in a hundred years, not since the Makers of Canada series. And yet every generation understands the past differently, and so sees in the mirror of these remarkable figures somewhat different lessons.

What strikes me again and again is just how dramatically ethical decisions figured in their lives. They form the backbone of history and memory. Some of these people, Big Bear, for example, or Dumont, or even Lucy Maud Montgomery, thought of themselves as failures by the end of their lives. But the ethical cord that was strung taut through their work has now carried them on to a new meaning and even greater strength, long after their deaths.

Each of these stories is a revelation of the tough choices unusual people must make to find their way. And each of us as readers will find in the desperation of the Chinese revolution, the search for truth in fiction, the political and military dramas, different meanings that strike a personal chord. At first it is that personal emotive link to such figures which draws us in. Then we find they are a key that opens the whole society of their time to us. Then we realize that in that 150-year period many of them knew each other, were friends, opposed each other. Finally, when all these stories are put together, you will see that a whole new debate has been created around Canadian civilization and the shape of our continuous experiment.

Take Nellie McClung, for example. We think of her as one of five—the one with a stage presence and a sense of humour. But Charlotte Gray reveals someone quite different. She can now be seen as the great strategist of the first wave of the women's movement and one of the most successful early feminists in the world. Why? Because she kept the movement mainstream and involved with broader issues, like the exploitation of immigrant women. When I read her story I discover a woman who today is still ahead of her time. I can imagine her speaking out right now on Iraq, on unsecured cheap labour, on the same old fat men controlling politics. I know she would make me laugh and make me want to help her change things for the better.

CHAPTER ONE

What Is So Great about Nellie?

Never retract, never explain, never apologize.
Get the thing done and let them howl.
MCCLUNG CAMPAIGN SLOGAN

Getting to know Nellie McClung over the past year has crystallized insights into Canadian women that have intrigued me ever since I arrived in this country in 1979. I have often noticed a sort of robust self-assurance exuded by women I've met here. And now I realize that Nellie has had a lot to do with this trait.

I noticed the confidence soon after I settled in Ottawa, and started to acquire a circle of women friends. In some respects—age, background, education—they were similar to the friends I had left behind in England. But as I got to know them better, I realized that, in subtle respects, they were quite different. It wasn't just that they were better cooks—perhaps because, back then, most Canadians were only one or two generations away from rural or small-town roots. It seemed to me that they had more confidence in their own opinions, and they were more self-assured about expressing them. They took themselves seriously, and they expected to be taken seriously.

What lay behind this sense of entitlement to their space in the world? I wondered. An obvious source was the egalitarianism that pervades Canada's public ethos—the assumption that anyone can make it up the ladder here. In 1979, this was a dramatic contrast to the class-ridden society I had left behind, where our accents and education betrayed the social niche into which we had been born. Another explanation for the difference was the Women's Movement, which in 1979 had had far more impact in North America than in Britain. Second-wave feminism had swept through my new Canadian friends' cohort while they were still in high school or university. The self-image of women had changed, and so had the way they related to men. Within Ottawa, my new home, political parties and the federal civil service were scrambling to recruit women. Not long after, this feminist tide also swept the land of my birth.

But I felt there was something else going on in Canada as well. Sure, women here had learned new political and social attitudes, but my new female friends already shared a conviction that the roles they played were as important in themselves as men's. What's more, the Canadian men I met often seemed to share that view.

All generalizations about human behaviour are dangerous, and there were plenty of exceptions on both sides of the Atlantic. The year I arrived here, 1979, was also the year that Britain voted for its first woman prime minister (Margaret Thatcher). Canada did not equal this advance for another decade and a half, and then for no longer than a blink of an eye: Kim Campbell was gone in months. And yet. . . .

Over the next few years, I immersed myself in Canadian literature. The women I met in books shared the sturdy self-image of my new Canadian friends. Novels and short stories by writers such as Carol Shields, Margaret Laurence, and Margaret Atwood often featured a particular archetype—a forthright, witty woman who was a dramatic contrast to the passive-aggressive women I met in British novels by the likes of Jane Austen, Elizabeth Bowen, and Penelope Lively. Then, in the mid-1990s, I started writing biographies of nineteenth-century Canadian women, including Isabel Mackenzie King (mother of Prime Minister King), the Mohawk poet Pauline Johnson, and those two resilient sisters Susanna Moodie and Catharine Parr Traill, who recorded their experiences in the backwoods of Canada. All these women fit the female Canadian archetype that I had already glimpsed in both modern Canadian literature and my own Canadian contemporaries.

Moodie and Traill, who arrived in Upper Canada as British immigrants in 1832 and whom I portrayed in *Sisters in the Wilderness*, best epitomize the determination and confidence of the archetype. These pioneer women displayed extraordinary courage, resourcefulness, and humour. It was their hard work, rather than that of their husbands, that kept their families afloat: they knew that they would survive only by their own efforts. One of my favourite quotes from Traill was her definition of what to do in an emergency: "It is folly to fold one's hands and sit down to bewail in abject terror: it is better to be up and doing."

At the other end of the nineteenth century, Nellie McClung belongs to the same tradition as those two redoubtable sisters. She too was a pragmatist who knew that survival in a harsh landscape depended on an individual's will to be "up and doing." As a child in the 1880s and 1890s, she watched her father breaking sod on the prairies, but she also recognized that her mother's efforts and determination played a crucial role in keeping the six children in the McClung family fed and healthy.

Like Moodie and Traill, Nellie chose to capture her experiences in print. She first established her reputation as the bestselling author of the novel *Sowing Seeds in Danny*. This wonderful portrait of small-town life in the West, published in 1908, has been undeservedly forgotten. But unlike Moodie and Traill, Nellie wanted to do more than write about the people she knew. She was an activist who wanted to improve society. Yes, there were folksy humour and quaint characters on the prairies, but there were also cruel gossip, drunken husbands, family abuse, and starving children. In the early years of the twentieth century, Nellie was already hard at work, making the personal political. She was a key figure in two of the critical campaigns of first-wave feminism: the fight to win the vote for women and (as a member of the Famous Five) the right of women to be considered "persons," and to be entitled to sit in the federal Senate.

Those achievements alone would be enough to earn Nellie McClung a place in our political pantheon. Her zest, her convictions, her campaigns helped shape the Canada we live in today. A prairie populist, she embodied the values that still characterize Canada—faith in government, a collective commitment to social programs. She altered the political landscape. However, success in both campaigns was a collective achievement: Nellie was not alone. She fought alongside other women—Cora Hind, Francis Beynon, Emily Murphy, Louise McKinney—who played a full part and shared the credit.

It is another aspect of Nellie McClung's career that has caught my attention, and which, I think, goes a long way to explaining the differences I noticed, nearly thirty years ago, between my British friends and my Canadian friends. It is also the reason that she is the pivotal feminist of first-wave feminism. Nellie's most important achievement was that she kept feminism mainstream, and she set the tone and pattern for the next century of women's political activity. Throughout the suffrage campaign and the Persons Case, she made sure that she did not marginalize herself or her views. Even as she challenged the status quo, she did not withdraw from the political centre into a third party that had little hope of forming a government.

Nellie McClung had seen with her own eyes that the Canadian west was settled by the combined efforts of both men and women, and that both genders deserved credit for what had been achieved in the face of daunting challenges. But in her view, the battles were never exclusively about women's rights. Even as she campaigned for a radical change in gender relations, she deliberately kept on board groups that were not obvious allies—immigrant women, farmers and their wives, working-class men, factory workers. Because of her childhood experiences as a homesteader, she had a broad and down-to-earth view of how society should operate, without discrimination against anyone—women, immigrants, Native people, Japanese Canadians, or strangers whose looks, accents, language, and gods differed from those of the dominant elite. Her egalitarianism set her apart from many of her fellow activists, who often shared the prejudices of their day.

Nellie was a tough fighter, but she was fair and she was funny. Indeed, in a country where we have always enjoyed mocking our politicians, her humour was absolutely essential to her success. (To rile her critics, she would quote a quip from her youngest son, "I am a suffragist's child and have never known a mother's love.") Nellie achieved with wit and irony what feminist leaders elsewhere achieved only with harsh rhetoric and demonstrations. She did this both as a bestselling author, threading feminist messages into her lively prose, and as a brilliant public speaker. Nellie McClung was the first Canadian woman who became famous as a political campaigner, and her reputation spread far beyond Canadian borders. The audiences who flocked to hear her speak absorbed her messages as they roared with laughter.

One cannot write about feminism without introducing a few heavy-handed references to patriarchy. Nellie was operating in a male-dominated society, and her actions did not dislodge the deeply rooted power structures of her Canada.

She never used the word herself, but by the time I arrived here references to "patriarchy" underlay every feminist analysis. They still do: society is slow to change. But I think that there is more gender equality in Canadian society than in any other country I have lived in (including Japan, Britain, and the United States), and I think in large measure we can thank Nellie McClung, the most important feminist of her time, for this.

CHAPTER TWO

Where Did Nellie Get the Nerve?

Ontario and Southern Manitoba, 1873–1892

> I do not want to pull through life like a thread
> that has no knot. I want to leave something
> behind when I go, some small legacy of truth,
> some word that will shine in a dark place.

We know almost too much about Nellie McClung's origins because she loved to tell the story herself. In two volumes of autobiography, and in details scattered through her novels and short stories, she recounts a tale rich in the raw material from which Canadian legends are made—a long trek, a log cabin, and bitter winters. Her account is a sentimental memoir of a vanished world, but along the way we can see some of the forces that shaped an engaging personality.

The beginning of the story is straightforward. The youngest of six children born to John and Letitia Mooney, on October 20, 1873, Nellie Letitia Mooney was seven years old when her parents made a momentous choice. Exhausted by the struggle to survive on their farm near Chatsworth, close to western Ontario's Bruce Peninsula, they decided to move west. The prairies' wide and golden horizons, the promise of rippling grasslands waiting for the plough, beckoned seductively. Almost every day, the Toronto *Globe* contained glowing reports in its "Latest From Manitoba" column. Nellie's mother, Letitia McCurdy, a stern Scots Presbyterian with an implacable sense of duty, was the one who pushed for the move, after her eldest son, William, then nineteen, had declared that anything would be better than scraping a threadbare existence from Grey County's cramped and stony fields. He was tired, he announced, of working on a treadmill. In the spring of 1879, Will set off for Manitoba, determined to stake a claim for land that would bear a decent crop. Nellie's father, John Mooney, an Irish Methodist with a genial wit and gentle smile, was less enthusiastic about leaving the 150 acres he had cleared himself. Twenty years older than his wife, he was now sixty-seven. His hands were gnarled and his back ached, and he had to ask himself, What was the point of starting all over again? But when a letter arrived from Will describing the land he had chosen, John was unable to resist the pressure from thin-lipped Letitia.

So a year after Will had headed west, the rest of Nellie's family packed up their belongings and set their faces toward the sunset. The journey they took is almost unimaginable in today's world of easy air connections and good roads. The Mooneys travelled for days—by steamship from Owen Sound across Lake Huron and Lake Superior to Duluth, Minnesota, then by train to St. Boniface, Manitoba, and finally in two heavily laden wagons pulled by oxen for two hundred kilometres west along a bone-bruising, rutted trail from Winnipeg. In September 1880 they arrived at the rough, unchinked log cabin, with one window and a thatched roof, that Will had built on the homestead he had staked out near the Souris River. Eight kilometres from the new town of Millford, Nellie's new home was set on shimmering meadows flowing around clumps of poplars. As soon as the Mooneys had unpacked an iron stove from their wagon, Letitia rolled up her sleeves and started baking bread.

During Nellie's first prairie winter, there were plenty of scares and panics: winds whistled, wolves howled, snow drifted, the cow died, and her sister Lizzie fell gravely ill. But Nellie's description of her family's pluck, in the face of loneliness, isolation, and hunger, is suffused with a constant undercurrent of cheerful optimism sustained by the Mooney faith that "God will provide." With the benefit of hindsight, she places herself in the centre of Canadian mythmaking—the struggle against the elements, culminating in the triumph of survival. When seeding time came that first spring, Nellie recalls walking "proudly behind my father in the clean new furrows in my bare feet, as he broke the new sod on our farm, and as the coulter cut the sod, and the share turned it over, I knew that he was doing something more than just plowing a field. I knew there was a significance in what he was doing, though I had no words to express it."

The significance was that John Mooney was part of a larger national endeavour in the late nineteenth century— peopling the prairies with homesteaders in the slow westward spread of the new Dominion of Canada. This was the "land of opportunity," in the words of government propaganda, and the Mooneys had grasped at the dream. However, achieving that dream was tough going. In 1880, there were fewer than sixty-six thousand settlers in Manitoba, and in the area where the Mooneys established themselves, there were no doctors, churches, schools, road signs, bridges. A handful of pioneer families like themselves lived hand-to-mouth in roughly built farmhouses, hoping others would settle on the empty acres around them. The Souris River valley itself was not part of Manitoba until a year after the Mooneys arrived, when the province's boundaries were extended. One of the biggest excitements in young Nellie's life came in 1882, when the Canadian Pacific Railway reached Brandon, forty kilometres away. The same year, John Mooney and his sons finally moved the family out of the one-room log house, with its prairie grass thatch roof, into a sturdy house with three bedrooms.

Nellie never downplayed the harshness of those early years on the prairie. As I read about "the sting of frost, and the horror of being lost in a blizzard," I reacted in exactly the way she intended—with an involuntary shiver. Nevertheless, she fell in love with the prairie landscape—the warm summer days when the sky was a cloudless azure arch over fields of yellow wheat; the crisp winter mornings when ice crystals glistened on the bare bushes; the purple twilights; the scent of pea vines and wolf willow blossom. Her memoirs glow with rosy nostalgia. "I was one of the children who found the pussy willows, and listened for the first meadow lark, and made little channels with a hoe to let the spring water find its way to the creek, and ran as swift as rabbits when the word went round that the ice was going out of the Souris, and cried if we missed it! I lay on the grassy banks in summer, and saw castles in the clouds, and dreamed great dreams of the future."

There were three sons and three daughters in the Mooney family. From the time they could walk, they each worked alongside their parents: pioneer farms required backbreaking labour from everybody. The three boys, William, George, and Jack, helped their father clear, plant, and harvest the land and care for the livestock. Nellie and her older sisters, Lizzie and Hannah, worked alongside Letitia as she washed, cooked, baked, sewed, churned, made candles and soap, preserved fruit and vegetables, salted pork, and raised livestock. It must have been a grind for her parents, but Nellie recalls life on the Mooney farm as a lark: "I distinctly remember that I had a very happy time working outside: that is, bringing up the cows, doing my share of the milking and particularly in harvest time I had the great joy of bringing out the lunch to the men. Occasionally I drove the horse rake to gather up the strands of grain the binder had missed. I never associated these things with the idea of work. In fact, I think if the bitter truth were told, I was not very fond of work, and I remember that when the dishes were coming up to be washed, my sister Hannah often remarked that I had a way of disappearing."

Nellie McClung's childhood under the wide Manitoba sky was all about fortitude and faith. She learned the importance of both hard work and a sense of community: neighbours looked out for one another in those days, knowing that there was nowhere else to turn when the plough broke, the flour bin was empty, or the baby was feverish. She inherited her father's Methodism, which allowed her to believe that a benevolent deity was looking out for her interests and that a dynamic faith could change society. She absorbed her mother's more severe Presbyterian absolutist views of right and wrong. (Letitia, adamant that one's soul must be stainlessly ready for Judgment Day, might have stepped straight out of a Victorian Gothic novel. One day, little Nellie opened her mother's bottom drawer and found a shroud, neatly folded in preparation for Letitia's inevitable death.) She attended community picnics where the band played "Rule Britannia," "The Maple Leaf," and "God Save the Queen."

Nellie always insisted that it was thanks to her upbringing that she developed a secure ego—an ego that, in the future, would withstand heartbreaking disappointment and public abuse. Her rural childhood, unsullied by concerns beyond the stark challenge of survival, meant that she had no time for urban insecurities about pedigree or class. This, she argued, was "one of the happiest circumstances of my life, for life [outside cities] is simple and sane, and normal, with a clear line drawn between right and wrong. . . . Country people have time to tidy up their minds, classify their emotions, and generally speaking, get their souls into shape. Personality develops more readily in the country, too, with its silences and its clear spaces which bring meditation to the heart!" The second crucial aspect of her childhood, she liked to acknowledge, was that she grew up in the certainty of being loved. "A person can face life better, can accomplish more, on the basis of a secure and happy childhood. I was a big girl before I knew that homes could ever break up. To me, home was the Rock of Gibraltar. That's a wonderful bulwark with which to face the world."

Yet a rural background and a rock-solid family don't begin to explain Nellie's subsequent successes. After all, her own siblings and hundreds of other bright kids in scattered prairie farmhouses enjoyed the same childhood, but it didn't turn them into powerful activists. The vast majority stayed close to their parents' homes and made their own lives on the prairies. What gave Nellie the nerve to challenge convention, work for social change, and become a national figure?

Some of the answers to this question are obvious. There was Nellie's own nature. As a child she was, to put it mildly, a handful. Her two older sisters, according to her descriptions, were much more docile. Elizabeth was "everybody's friend," and Hannah "spoke only when she had something to say." Nellie also had a wicked sense of humour: her success at making people laugh gave her a taste for the limelight. As the youngest child, Nellie occupied a very particular space in her large, close-knit family: she was the baby indulged by brothers William and George and her father (who, despite Letitia's disapproval, loved her cheeky mimicry of his wife's spinster aunts). And as the smallest member of the family, she was also quick (too quick, in the view of her brook-no-nonsense mother) to assert her rights against her siblings. She wanted to know why her brother Jack, only four years her senior, was allowed far more freedom. She wanted to know why she had to wear long skirts that prevented her competing in races against boys at the community picnic. She was furious when Letitia wouldn't let her run in her underwear, but when she demanded a reason, she met only "a stone wall . . . that baffled me."

Nellie wasn't just mouthy for the sake of it. Here's where nurture kicks in. The seeds of the progressive liberalism that would become the hallmark of Nellie's views were planted in her by her parents and their friends. From an early age she overheard complaints about eastern politicians, who were so slow to make the investment in infrastructure that the prairie farmers needed. The prairie grasslands were rapidly being replaced by a checkerboard of fields in which Red Fife wheat grew. But getting the grain to eastern markets was a problem. The nearest elevator for the Mooney grain was in Brandon, which meant a long drive with a loaded wagon, a long wait at the elevator, and then (according to disgruntled local farmers) long odds that they would be shortchanged on its value. Why wasn't there a branch line from Brandon to Souris? And if the Canadian Pacific Railway was too busy forging a steel spine across the continent toward its Pacific destination, why shouldn't another railway company, even an American one, build a branch line? (The CPR finally opened a Brandon–Souris line in 1886.)

Eastern businessmen were just as bad as the politicians. Thanks to the tariff system, prairie farmers were forced to buy made-in-Ontario harvesters rather than less expensive American machinery manufactured in the Midwest, even though the Canadian machines were not designed for vast prairie fields. Farmers lost valuable harvest days when the machines broke down, and spare parts were unavailable. John Mooney was too much an old Ontario Tory to join the newly formed Farmers' Protective Union of Manitoba, established in 1883. But his weary sighs of exasperation affected his youngest daughter.

Perhaps the most significant individual in Nellie's intellectual development was a young man called Frank Schultz, who in 1883 was appointed teacher at the newly built Northfield

School, three kilometres from the Mooney farm. Nellie had reached her tenth birthday unable to read, because up until then the nearest schoolhouse was half a day's walk away. This must have irked her mother, who had a Scots reverence for education but had had no time to teach Nellie herself. Nellie loved the story of how a neighbour had once suggested to Letitia Mooney that education was wasted on girls who should be "patchin' quilts" rather than reading books. Letitia Mooney gave the neighbour a black look. "Every child has a right to an education and if you do not get that for them, you have cheated them."

Nellie's account of her first day at school is vintage McClung—an uplifting tale of adversity overcome. When she confessed her illiteracy to Mr. Schultz, he gave her a reassuring smile and told her she would be reading within three months. "The compact was sealed," she wrote over fifty years later. "I knew my burden of ignorance was going to be lifted. . . . A new world had opened before me. Another door had opened!"

Frank Schultz did more for Nellie than open a door to literacy. He also taught her to think for herself, and to question conventional wisdom. In 1884, the homesteaders in southern Manitoba were unsettled by some worrying news. Louis Riel, who had led the 1870 Métis uprising against the government in Ottawa, had returned from his self-imposed exile in Montana and was stirring up trouble in Saskatchewan. The Mooneys' friends anxiously exchanged rumours about raids on non-Native settlers, and about the fiery leader's appeal to local Cree and Blackfoot. "Why don't they arrest him now, and get him safely in jail before someone is killed?" Letitia Mooney exclaimed at one get-together. A neighbour was indignant that the federal government had not acted. "Red coats and a flash of steel" would settle Riel's grievances, he said, adding that Louis Riel should have been hanged ten years earlier for the murder of Ontario Orangeman Thomas Scott.

None of the adults in the Mooneys' parlour that night challenged this opinion. But Nellie, alongside her sister Hannah, did. "Mr. Schultz had told us about [this] in school. The half-breeds and the Indians had a grievance, a real one. The settlers were crowding in on them. . . . I knew the government was to blame." Both girls repeated what Mr. Schultz had told them—how the country had originally belonged to the Aboriginal peoples, how the government surveyors were disrupting the Métis' traditional landholding arrangements, how Ottawa had been dismissive of their grievances. Letitia Mooney was horrified to hear such subversive arguments from her daughters. A farmer from down the road told Hannah that in Russia, "you would be shot for a Nihilist, my girl." Hannah quietly continued to wipe the dinner dishes, but Nellie wouldn't shut up. In her autobiography, she describes how she passionately argued that the situation of the Métis paralleled that of farmers. Just as farm implement manufacturers ignored the legitimate complaints of people like her father, so Ottawa ignored the legitimate Métis grievances. Her impudence and her arguments, she recorded with glee, outraged her audience. She was less gleeful the following year, when the Métis uprising was brutally crushed and Louis Riel was hanged in the icy jail yard of the Mounted Police barracks in Regina.

THE MOONEY SONS were happy to remain on the land: William and George were soon established on farms close to their parents' acreage. Elizabeth married a local farmer. But both Hannah and Nellie wanted more. Nellie railed against the constraints of her childhood: the hand-me-down clothes, the "acid little economies" imposed by Letitia Mooney (which included no oil for lamps after homework was finished, so no bedtime reading). She also resented her mother's rigid views on "proper" behaviour for girls, her "Old-world reverence for men," and her constant disapproval of Nellie's impulse to be "forward" and "too free with her tongue." A great self-dramatist, Nellie wallowed in her dissatisfaction. "In my fiercest moods of rebellion, I was glad of these irritations; they kept alive my ambition. I would make my escape; I would gain my independence, and every day brought me nearer."

But how to escape? There was only one route for young women like her: education. Education offered a path out of rural poverty for women: if she qualified as a schoolteacher, she could support herself if she remained unmarried, or supplement the family income if the man she married hit hard times. Sweet-natured Hannah had already chosen this career, and spent six months at the teachers' college, then known as "normal school," in Winnipeg. In July 1889, Nellie Mooney learned that she too had passed the normal school admission exams. The five months she spent at "the normal" were, she always said, "pure delight" as she plunged into subjects like psychology, the history of education, and school management. Her own ignorance made her self-conscious. When her fellow students talked of "Charlemagne, Ivanhoe and Sairy Gamp, I had to sit silent and ashamed." But Nellie Mooney never sat silent for long. Besides, there was the new world of a big city to discover. Winnipeg boasted horse-drawn streetcars, drugstores with green and red bottles in their windows, bookstores bursting with new publications and sheet music. Nellie drank it all in—especially the glimpses of the city's aristocracy, "party dresses held up daintily, showing fur boots on little feet." Despite the distractions, Nellie Mooney had earned her teacher's certificate by the following February, when she was sixteen years old. She had also absorbed several valuable lessons from Mr. Goggin, the normal school principal: to love righteousness and eschew evil, to wash frequently, and to wear clean linen. Mr. Goggin also urged his students to stand up for themselves and "demand decent salaries." He knew how often timid youngsters were exploited and how unstable a teacher's life could be. In the next five years, Nellie would teach in four different schools.

Nellie Mooney's first job was in the little Manitoba town of Hazel, near Manitou, 120 kilometres east of the Mooney homestead. Her new kingdom boasted a blackboard, a map of the world largely coloured British Empire pink, and a potbellied wood-burning stove. The first day, forty students, some the same age as Nellie herself, filed into the one-room schoolhouse, with its acrid smell of chalk dust, carbolic acid, and unwashed humanity. By the end of the first week, Nellie had learned their names and divided them up into eight grades. She was an excellent teacher: as one of her pupils recalled, "she had a way of inciting a child to try harder all the time and to achieve." Success reinforced Nellie's sense that she could control her own destiny.

In the first volume of her autobiography, *Clearing in the West*, Nellie McClung uses all the devices of formula fiction—foreshadowing, adversity followed by epiphany— to keep her reader entranced. Her description of those early weeks in Hazel includes mention of the preacher's wife, a graceful, square-faced woman with golden brown eyes, wearing a velvet bonnet, who arrived to teach the Sunday school. Nellie describes how she was dazzled by this apparition, and how she made the extraordinary announcement that "she is the only woman I have ever seen whom I should like to have for a mother-in-law." When she later discovered that this ethereal creature had a red-haired son who was working in the local drugstore, she took action. "I made no pretense of being the Victorian maiden who sits on the shore waiting for a kindly tide to wash something up at her feet—not at all! Having seen something that looked like a treasure, I plunged boldly in and swam out for it!"

The "treasure" was Wesley McClung, a qualified pharmacist who would become her husband. Nellie put on her dark green, brass-buttoned Sunday best dress, shone her shoes with lard and lamp black, and made a special trip to the Manitou drugstore to inspect him. She spent her last three dollars on a fountain pen—after she had insisted that this "treasure" first demonstrate every model available.

Did Nellie's romance with Wes really begin this way? I'm skeptical that a sixteen-year-old picked her mother-in-law before she met her beau. Like every memoirist, Nellie shapes her story with the benefit of hindsight, and her delight in a good tale frequently distorts the truth. She is a storyteller, relying on sequence and causality to give coherence to the messy, inchoate details of her years as a child growing up in a close-knit family. Yet, as her biographer, I admit that Nellie has at least as much right as I do to a particular version of the turning points in her life. Who can tell whether a handful of carefully selected incidents and circumstances—the stability of the Mooney family, the arrival of a gifted teacher at Northfield School—really are the keys to Nellie's assertive personality and later fame? A biographer is also a storyteller, imposing order, economy, and moral consequence on the helter-skelter wash of her subject's experiences. There must have been dozens of other influences and events that went unrecorded, and are now lost to history. How many of those were equally significant?

I can only speculate. But a photograph of Nellie, taken when she was nineteen, gives some insight into the young woman she had become. The velvet bow that perches on top of the knot of thick, dark, unruly curls and the elegant, creamy, high-necked lace blouse that frames her face suggest an individual determined to please the eye. The direct gaze of the dark, deep-set eyes indicates a character unafraid to speak her mind, while the smile that plays on the half-open lips suggests easy recourse to laughter. The most striking feature, however, is the angle of Nellie's chin. The photographer caught Nellie in half-profile, looking off to his left, with her dimpled chin thrust firmly forward. Lively and good-looking, Nellie McClung radiates self-assurance and an appetite for life. In the future, I can see that people will cross this woman at their own peril. The woman in the photograph has a lot of nerve.

CHAPTER THREE

Why Write?

Manitou, 1892–1907

> I wanted to write, and how could I write
> unless I lived and felt, and sorrowed, and
> living was dangerous.

By the time she reached her seventeenth birthday, Nellie McClung was well launched in the profession of school-teacher—the classic female escape route from family and domestic drudgery. But her ambitions were not confined to drumming the three Rs into the heads of rowdy country kids. Since the moment she herself had finally learned to read, there had been another dream. She wanted to write.

It took all of her nerve to believe that she could be a writer. Even though she was a qualified teacher, she had only six years of schooling. She had never met a writer. Books were scarce on pioneer homesteads. "No one knows what books can mean except those of us who have been hungry for them," Nellie later remarked. "The depth of my ignorance appalled me. . . . What did I know of the world's great literature?" The little she knew came from a variety of sources. There were a few European classics on the Northfield School shelves, including such Victorian stalwarts as *Swiss Family Robinson*, *Twenty Thousand Leagues Under the Sea*, and *Ivanhoe*. Newcomers to the district were interrogated about what books they had brought with them: an English hired hand supplied Charles Kingsley's *Westward Ho!* and Fanny Burney's *Evelina*. Nellie also managed to get her hands on poetry by Milton and Longfellow and back issues of *A Girl's Own Annual*. A mysterious English benefactor called Miss M.E. Breasted sent the Mooneys a package of newspapers and books at regular intervals for ten years.

Once she had learned to read, Nellie's weekly pick-me-up was the serialized romantic novels in a publication prized by farming families across Canada: the Montreal *Family Herald*. It was valued for both what it said and what it did: when everybody had read it, each page was carefully snipped into four and hung in the outhouse. Every Saturday, Nellie collected a bundle of the previous week's issues of the *Family Herald* from the post office in Millford, eight kilometres away. Then she would dawdle home with her nose buried in its pages.

However, these books and serials had nothing to do with life on the Canadian prairies in the 1880s: the heroes were usually wealthy and titled, and the heroines flaunted ringlets, petticoats, and a tendency to faint clean away. The lack of reality in Nellie's reading matter was reflected in one of her first literary creations—a tearful, and misspelt, obituary verse:

> Four dead dogs—they died alone.
> Nobody saw them or heard them grown [sic],
> There they died by the drifts of snow,
> While the wind rocked their tales [sic] to and fro.

Hannah Mooney protested to her little sister that the whole thing was a fantasy, since the family did not have four dogs, and "a person shouldn't lie, even in an epitaph." But Nellie had a point: if her reading matter was so disconnected from her own life, why shouldn't her stabs at writing be equally surreal?

Today, one marvels that the prairie youngster was so hell-bent on becoming a writer. Why? In memoirs written in later years, she gives several reasons. She nursed an escapist inclination, on behalf of others as well as herself. "I want to give people release from their drab lives!" she recalls telling a young friend. "This is not all of the life—this sowing and reaping, cooking and washing dishes. There is an inner life that can be deepened and widened." The adult Nellie also claimed a budding desire to bridge that gap between "literature" and real life, and capture the experience of pioneer life that nobody else was recording. Her greatest literary discovery was Charles Dickens, and after immersing herself in the miseries of Oliver Twist and Pip, she decided she wanted to "do for the people around me what Dickens had done for his people." This was a literary urge, to "be a voice for the voiceless as he had been a defender of the weak . . . to make people understand each other; to make the commonplace things divine."

And there was another, more basic impulse to Nellie's dreams. Although her mother reprimanded her for being too forward, and her brother Jack constantly accused her of "showing off," she yearned for the limelight. Writing, like teaching, was one of the few avenues into a public life open to women like Nellie in late nineteenth-century Canada. Local newspapers regularly carried poetry and short stories by women. The Mooney family was unlikely to know that these were also the years when women were pushing their way into less welcoming professions. Dr. Emily Stowe had hung out her shingle in Toronto in 1880, the first female physician to do so in Canada, while the brilliant geneticist

Dr. Carrie Derrick was appointed the first female instructor at Montreal's McGill University in 1892. However, these trailblazers—considered aberrations by most observers—were urban middle-class women armed against male hostility by education and social standing. Nellie had none of those advantages, and Manitoba offered few opportunities for professional or artistic advancement. The University of Manitoba was founded only three years before the Mooneys' arrival in the province, and the closest thing to a provincial music scene was raucous renderings of the ballad "Remember the Red River Valley" at church picnics. "We had no telephones, picture-shows, radios, phonographs, daily papers or lending libraries," Nellie recalls in *Clearing in the West*. But the cultural shortcomings of her background were irrelevant to Nellie: she had a good imagination and a hunger for attention. She captures this ambition when she records her fifteen-year-old self's melodramatic announcement to a fellow student at teachers' college: "I want to get a toehold on the ladder of literature."

Today, at the touch of a TV remote control or a keyboard, we can track political events, converse with distant teachers, order the latest Canadian bestseller, log onto a dating service, or watch the same soap operas as people on another continent. In contrast, an ambitious young woman like Nellie was both isolated and doubly peripheral. She lived in a sparsely populated province far from the cultural centres of her young country—a country itself overshadowed by the great empire of which it was part. A few indigenous poets were starting to get published in Toronto—university-educated men like Bliss Carman and Archibald Lampman who romanticized Canada's landscapes and lakes. But Canada's educated elite during these years was more interested in Oscar Wilde's decadent Grosvenor Gallery goings-on in London than in a nascent Canadian literature—let alone the grimy struggles of prairie lives.

Yet there is one aspect of Nellie's life with which we can empathize—a dilemma as real for young women today as it was for her in the 1890s. She was torn between the urge to make her mark on the world, and the dream of a husband and family. The tension between these two ambitions occupied most of her twenties. In 1892, after eighteen months teaching in Hazel, she moved to the four-room school in Manitou, a lively community of eight hundred residents about six kilometres away. Manitou was a rural centre of growing importance: it had five grain elevators, a pump factory, a creamery, a flour mill, and no fewer than four churches, three hotels, and two weekly newspapers. But the highlight of the move, for Nellie Mooney, was that she was to board with the Methodist minister's family—the family that included the graceful Sunday school teacher who had enraptured her at Hazel and the pharmacist who had sold her a fountain pen, plus two more sons and a daughter. Reverend J.A. McClung, the minister, was quite a character, with his bushy white beard and eyebrows and "all the conquering fire of the circuit rider." However, it was his wife, Annie E. McClung, whose "fearless, radical mind" and unconventional attitudes to gender roles caught Nellie's attention. The McClung household was so different from the one that Nellie had grown up in. The two younger McClung boys were expected to take their turn at dishwashing and bed making along with their sister, Eleanor. Eleanor McClung did not have to be accompanied everywhere by one of her brothers. And what were the new boarder's feelings about Wes McClung—the red-haired eldest son who worked long hours in the local drugstore? "While I was still profoundly serious in my determination to travel the highway of life alone, giving myself to the world of letters, I liked this tall slim young man of twenty very well indeed."

Manitou offered Nellie new experiences, and she grabbed them. She took lessons in music and painting; she went to well-chaperoned dances on Friday nights organized by local service clubs; she spent Saturday afternoons in a reading room newly opened by the Women's Christian Temperance Union. The WCTU was a force to be reckoned with in North America in the late nineteenth century. Originally established in the northern United States in 1874, it had rapidly spread throughout Canada because drunkenness was a serious problem everywhere. (In the beer parlours of Victorian Canada, the initials were said to stand for "Women Continually Torment Us.")

At this stage, Nellie was less interested in petitions and pledges than in the debates that the Manitou branch of the WCTU sponsored. Each Saturday afternoon, she would put on her best dress, tie her long brown hair into a neat knot, take a deep breath, and sally forth to debate ideas with women twice her age. "We argued on annexation with the United States or the relative value of science and literature in schools, or whether or not it is possible to live without sin." Her descriptions of these debates remind me of modern book clubs—congenial all-female affairs where women give public expression to their opinions, without male onlookers to inhibit them. Nellie, the teacher and natural performer, revelled in them: she learned to be forceful without being rude, and to know what she wanted to say before she opened her mouth. So what if discussions took place in a dusty room over a noisy restaurant, and the watery coffee was served in chipped white cups? "We felt that we were living in the best tradition of the coffee houses of London."

By now, Wes McClung owned the drugstore in Manitou, which had a four-room apartment on the second floor. In her autobiography, Nellie describes the development of her relationship with Wes McClung as if it were a painless evolution from friendship to marriage. "I knew I could be happy with Wes. We did not always agree but he was a fair fighter, and I knew I would rather fight with him than agree with anyone else. I would not be afraid of life with him." She leaves the impression that there was no tension between marriage and her literary aspirations. "I would not need to lay aside my ambition if I married him. He would not want me to devote my whole life to him, he often said."

I know that the older Nellie was kidding herself, and her readers, when she wrote this. I've read extracts from a diary she kept intermittently at the time, in which she admitted far more confusion and doubt. Sometimes she was ecstatic that she had "the greatest gift on God's earth, a happy and requited love." Other times she was utterly miserable: "When you cry with dry eyes, and a quiet mouth, and a sore heart—that hurts." School boards rarely accepted married teachers, so marriage meant the end of teaching. What about those literary aspirations? In her notebook, she wrote sadly of her younger self: "So full of ambition and the desire to excel. . . . O, the high hopes, the daydreams of greatness and fame, never, never to be realized. . . . I was to have been a great author . . . and sway the minds of many and hear the whole world ring with my praise." Her friends echoed her doubts. One friend to whom she confided her marriage plans was shocked. "But you planned to be a *writer*, Nellie," the young woman protested.

Somehow, Wes McClung managed to reassure Nellie. Perhaps it was his stolid good sense that attracted impulsive young Nellie. (One mutual friend described Wes's equable temperament in a wonderfully idiosyncratic phrase: he was a man, she said, who "can do a lot of washing in a very few suds.") Perhaps Nellie herself, despite her ambitions, couldn't face becoming that most dreary of all Victorian stereotypes, "an old maid." She was twenty-three years old now—late to marry by the standards of the time. Her sharp-tongued mother gave her own verdict on the pharmacist: "You have more sense than I ever gave you credit for," Letitia tartly told her youngest daughter. "I like your young man—I couldn't have picked out a finer one myself. Now, if you cannot get on, I'll be inclined to think it will be your fault." On August 25, 1896, Wes and Nellie McClung were married in Wawanesa Presbyterian Church (the Methodist church was too small) close to her parents' farm. As the newlyweds boarded the train to return to Manitou, a passing storm spattered them with rain and nearly blew Nellie's hat away. The squall allowed Nellie's romantic streak to let rip when she later described that journey at the end of her first volume of autobiography. While Wes and his bride stood on the back platform of the little steam train, the wind died down and the clouds parted. "It was clearing in the West!" wrote Nellie, with the hindsight of forty years of marriage. "Tomorrow would be fine!"

Women had almost no control over their fertility in the late nineteenth century: the term "birth control" was coined only in 1914, and contraception was not legalized in Canada until 1969. Primitive methods of birth control, such as thick condoms, were available under the counter at pharmacies, and there was surreptitious discussion of vinegar pessaries and *coitus interruptus*. Wes, as a pharmacist, would have known all this, but I suspect that he never raised this taboo subject with his ingenuous young bride. If he had done so, I don't think Nellie would have woken up feeling queasy only two months after the wedding. She focused her sudden rush of resentment and despair on her physical discomfort: "Why had not something been found to save women from this infernal nausea? . . . If it had been a man's disease, it would have been made the subject of scientific research and relieved long ago. But women could suffer: it kept them humble! . . . Life at that moment looked like a black conspiracy against women." At that moment, I suspect, Nellie McClung was wailing about vanishing dreams of independence as well as her churning stomach.

There were also the dangers of childbirth to consider. All births took place at home during these years, with a midwife in attendance or (more rarely) a doctor. Everybody in Manitou knew of families where a young wife had died in childbirth after hours of painful labour, or a baby had arrived stillborn. The local undertaker always kept a supply of small coffins ready. But the McClungs' first son, Jack, was born safely at dawn on June 16, 1897, after an easy labour. Nellie's hesitations dissolved instantly: the first time her firstborn was laid next to her was "the most exquisite moment I have ever known." Jack was followed eighteen months later by Florence, then Paul in November 1900, then Horace in June 1906. A fourth son, Mark, arrived in 1911, when Nellie was thirty-eight. Nellie found motherhood absorbing and thrilling. She loved the smell of her infants and their chubby limbs as they grew, and she quickly adopted the view that a mother's first duty was to her own children. But motherhood also aroused a crusading urge. She announced that "the woman who really loves her own children . . . is the woman that wants to see other people's children get their chance too. . . . Women must be made to feel their responsibility. All this protective love, this instinctive mother love, must be organized some way, and made effective." Strong maternal instincts, she decided, should be channelled into social reforms that would improve conditions for all children. She listed slum conditions, malnourishment, child labour, and drunkenness as the obvious targets of women's organizations like the WCTU. "I determined that I would stir the deep waters of complacency."

During her children's infancy, Nellie was almost submerged in childrearing routines—nursing, housekeeping, childhood illnesses, Sunday school picnics. "I did not spend much time studying world happenings." She always had household help—a local girl during the early years, and a succession of young foreign women later. And despite the diapers and drudgery, she never lost her determination to write. Two weeks after her wedding, a good-looking young man had appeared at her door with the prospectus for a new monthly magazine, to be called *Town and Country*. Each issue would profile the leading citizens of a chosen town. Manitou had been selected for the first issue, and several people had suggested that the pharmacist's wife was the ideal person to write some of the sketches. Was Mrs. McClung interested?

It was a scam. The charming young man relieved Nellie
of five dollars for a magazine subscription, and was never
heard of again. But before Nellie realized she'd been swin-
dled, she threw herself into her writing assignment—poring
over the *Manitou Mercury* newspaper files, investigating
local businesses, and interviewing people at great length. On
breezy, clear afternoons she would stride along rutted farm
tracks to distant farms, where she would be invited into the
kitchen for a mug of tea. Nellie was a good listener, and
farmers' wives poured out their hearts to this sympathetic
young woman who scribbled down their life stories while
she ate their homemade squares. Some speakers nursed
healthy babies as they spoke about the peaceful routines of
rural life, and the thrill of putting down roots in a new country. But other careworn wives pleated aprons anxiously
between their fingers as they admitted to desperate loneliness, or confided anguish triggered by successive miscar-
riages, drunken husbands, abusive relationships, ruined
harvests, or dashed hopes. The anecdotes she gathered, and
her insights into homesteaders' lives, would later find their
way into her fiction. "I really did learn something about the
people of the community, and got a glimpse of their hopes
and fears and their ambitions for their children." The exer-
cise also made her a more critical reader, analyzing how

authors as varied as the American short story writer Bret
Harte and the English novelist George Eliot achieved their
impact on readers. "I never regretted the time I spent getting
material for *Town and Country*, for I felt it was not wasted."

Despite domestic demands, Nellie grabbed every opportunity to write. She composed advertisements for the prod-
ucts in Wes's drugstore for the local papers. ("From Cough
to Coffin," read one jingle, which included the ditty "Wet
feet / Bad cold / Hacking cough / Churchyard mould / Thus
in brief the story's told," before going on to extol "Scarlett's
Cough Cure . . . Try a bottle—Stay your flight.") Once she
even won five dollars for composing a slogan for Stearns
Headache Powders: "I bought a washing machine with the
money," she noted. She sent off so many verses and short
stories to the Canadian Methodist Sunday school paper that
its editor, Dr. William H. Withrow, issued a polite protest:
"I have enough on hand for some time."

It was Annie McClung who gave Nellie the kind of help
that a budding author with four children underfoot really
needs. In 1902, her mother-in-law pointed out to Nellie a
short story contest sponsored by the popular American magazine *Colliers Weekly*. Nellie, now twenty-nine, was fired up—
but how could she afford the time? There was the church tea to
organize, a child's dress to sew. . . . Annie brooked no excuses.

"If you wait until you are ready to write, you will never write." She put aside her own activities and took over the household for a day, while Nellie sat down and wrote the first draft of a short story. The main character was an endearing young girl called Pearlie Watson, who looked after her little brother Danny. The story did not win the *Colliers Weekly* contest, but Nellie then sent it to Dr. Withrow. She heard nothing for almost three years. Then, in June 1905, a mysterious letter arrived from one "E.S.C." praising the story's "vitality, humour and originality." The manuscript had found its way to the William Briggs's Methodist Book and Publishing House in Toronto, where editor Edward Caswell decided that Nellie should "go ahead with this and make it into a book." By the following spring, Caswell had the full manuscript in his hands.

"Dear Mrs. McClung," he wrote on April 26, 1906. "Tonight at home I got my first chance at a good read of this story of yours—and I finished it up. I can hardly describe to you the sensations or emotions it evoked. It is a wonderful story. . . . I don't know when a story moved me more. . . . And yet through my tears, I found myself bursting into a chuckle over some of your inimitable touches of humour."

Nellie's first novel, *Sowing Seeds in Danny*, was finally published in July 1908, by William Briggs in Canada and

Doubleday in the United States. By then, Nellie had the literary wind in her sails: she had written short stories for several Canadian and U.S. magazines, including *Saturday Night*, the *Delineator*, the *Canadian Home Journal*, and the *Ladies' Home Journal*. Her first novel was a Canadian best-seller within two months of publication. She was one of only two Canadian authors to appear on the *Bookseller and Stationer's* list of American bestsellers for the previous six years. The other was fellow Manitoban Ralph Connor, with whom she shared a focus on the importance and dignity of ordinary folk. Readers embraced young Pearlie Watson, who held her poverty-stricken family together through force of character and sturdy humour. Nellie McClung's powerful mix of gentle satire and shrewd insights into human behaviour engaged both male and female readers. Westerners revelled in the chance to read about their own world—the dramas of pioneer life on a harsh and beautiful prairie landscape—rather than the worlds of bewigged English aristocrats or sooty-faced Londoners. Now thirty-five, Nellie had achieved the goal she had spoken of when she was fifteen: she had a toehold on the ladder of literature.

There would be two more volumes about Pearlie Watson after *Sowing Seeds in Danny*, and a further thirteen books of autobiography, poetry, fiction, and collected essays and columns, many of which were bestsellers during her lifetime. In addition, Nellie published dozens of short stories, articles, and opinion columns in newspapers and magazines. But her greatest creation was Pearlie Watson—a real original, who deserves comparison with another all-Canadian character who emerged the same year, in Lucy Maud Montgomery's *Anne of Green Gables*. Both red-haired Anne and plain-speaking Pearlie behaved and thought like real little girls; both stories were set on vividly described regional landscapes; both appealed to a readership eager for something other than British stereotypes. A century after its publication, *Sowing Seeds in Danny* is still a lively, fun read that includes fascinating details about life in a small pioneer town.

Nellie earned a respectable income from her pen—an income that would be of increasing importance to McClung family fortunes. But she never won the lasting international recognition as an author that L.M. Montgomery achieved. Most of Nellie's fiction is "too loaded with nineteenth century sentimentality to hold the attention of a modern reader," as Norah Story, author of *The Oxford Companion to Canadian History and Literature*, puts it. Although Nellie liked to describe herself as an author, her writing seldom got 100 percent of her attention: she dashed off most of her books in one draft, between lecture tours and political meetings.

Recently, the German poet and scholar Klaus Martens has accused Nellie of plagiarism. In a collection he edited of correspondence by the prairie author Frederick Philip Grove, Martens quotes an indignant 1925 letter in which Grove, then a little-known writer, says that Nellie "simply clips passages from *The Turn of the Year* [his fictionalized memoir published in 1923] and twists their tail" in her novel *Painted Fires*, published in 1925. Grove was notoriously thin-skinned, and Nellie certainly did not lift whole paragraphs of prose from his memoir. She may not have even realized that a few of her phrases echo Grove's (she blithely told him that she kept a copy of his book on her desk, and had learned much from his descriptions of nature). But she certainly recognized some of her shortcomings as a novelist. She could rarely bring herself to give readers anything other than a happy ending: "I see no good in a book that teaches that life is a hopeless mess." She specialized in recounting anecdotes and turning them into parables. Her later fiction often slid into propaganda for one of her causes—Prohibition, women's rights, pacifism, welfare programs. "I believe a writer must have a vision of a better world if his work is to live," she insisted, as she churned out morally uplifting tales in which vigorous, brave women shame men into behaving better.

Nonetheless, Nellie was a committed and important writer. She wrote because she was a born storyteller and she felt compelled to write. She couldn't help herself, she *needed* an outlet for her imagination and creativity. She wanted to write about people whom her own neighbours would recognize, and at the same time she wanted to expose injustice.

Once her first book was published, she had an additional reason to write. Literary success opened new doors for her. She started giving dramatic public readings from *Sowing Seeds in Danny*, and invitations began to trickle in, first from all over Manitoba, and then from Ontario and the northern United States. Soon the trickle became a flood, and Nellie evolved from reader to speaker. Her own vivacious warmth merged with her heroine's as she offered Pearlie's philosophy of life: "You, too, can do it." In 1910, the Brandon *Sun* reported, "Even to those who were well-acquainted with Mrs. McClung's ability as a reader, her work on last evening's program was a pleasing surprise. Instead of reading from the text, she gave her numbers entirely from memory, and her interpretation of the five chapters given revealed histrionic talent of a high order." Nellie had discovered her métier: public speaking. Writing was her way of recruiting an audience—an audience she could then enlist for her campaigns for social justice.

CHAPTER FOUR

What Got Her So Fired Up?

Manitou, 1907–1910

> The abduction of a young girl is punishable by five years' imprisonment but the stealing of a cow is punished by a fourteen-year sentence. Property has ever been held dearer than flesh and blood when the flesh and blood are woman's.

As we gaze back across the years, there are some aspects about Nellie's era that are almost incomprehensible to us. One is the position of women. So great is the change effected by the Women's Movement over the past century that today we cannot grasp the absolute nonstatus of women a hundred years ago. It was not simply a question of women being denied the vote, denied education, and denied professional status—but in all other respects being regarded as responsible human beings. When Nellie was a young teacher, women had *no* legal protections. We were regarded as a lesser level of humanity—

and back then, the majority of women themselves implicitly shared this view. An unmarried woman stayed beneath the protection of her father or brother. In the eyes of the law, married women existed only as wives, or not at all. Abortion was totally illegal and rarely discussed. If a woman was trapped in an unhappy marriage, she was not only blamed for her "failure" as a wife, but if she left her husband she had little hope of getting a fair share of her husband's estate or reasonable child support. If her husband decided he wanted to keep the children with him, she had no legal right to contest him. Today, the reality of life for women with no legal protections is beyond our frame of reference—until, perhaps, we see contemporary pictures of heavily veiled women in the repressive regimes of Iran or Afghanistan.

In Manitou, Nellie frequently saw the utter helplessness of women. Dejected wives and downtrodden daughters crop up again and again in her fiction as exhausted, sad characters, their health ruined by drudgery, annual pregnancies, or spousal abuse. "Winter-killed souls" she called these broken-spirited women, and she described their predicament with gentle irony and biting satire. In one short story, Annie Berry "died from overwork and child-bearing." But all her husband, Luke, could say was, "Women don't seem to have the sand in them they used to have; my mother raised fifteen and lost five, and I have often heard my father say they never had a doctor in the house and never needed one." Nellie added, poker-faced, "It was quite evident that Luke Berry had been badly treated."

In Nellie's fiction, the only weapon a woman has in the world is her own courage. She loved writing stories about spirited young women (most of whom resemble her) who transcend the barriers and prejudices they face through sheer force of character. But there were plenty of women without her heroines' spunk, and the reality of their lives— the hardship and helplessness—deeply offended Nellie McClung's strong sense of natural justice. The vulnerability of women, and the failure of the state to protect them, sparked a slow burn inside her. Why was it, Nellie wondered one day, that homesteaders always left their land to their sons, regardless of what their daughters had contributed in labour? She knew of one family in which each son had inherited a full section of land. The equally deserving daughter received one hundred dollars and a cow named Bella. "How would you like to be left at forty years of age, with no training and very little education, facing the world with one hundred dollars and one cow, even if she were named Bella?" Nellie asked, in a line that even a famous satirist like Mark Twain could not improve on.

Nellie McClung wanted to make a difference within her world: she wanted to eradicate the injustices she saw. But the starting point for Nellie's campaigns to improve women's lives is one that strikes a modern reader as a curious place to begin. When she was not talking about Pearlie Watson, she was usually speaking about the dangers of alcohol. Why did she begin there?

Today, we assume that the obvious solutions to women's powerlessness were twentieth-century reforms—greater access to education, well-paid employment, political power, and laws that recognized gender equality. But when Nellie was growing up in Manitoba, such ideas were unthinkable for most people she knew, including her own mother, Letitia Mooney. The idea that a woman's primary role in life was to be anything other than wife and mother was as startling to Letitia as the notion that one day human beings would walk on the moon.

This was where the Women's Christian Temperance Union came in. Women like Letitia could see that many women were desperately badly treated, and they could also see that alcohol was often part of the problem. Too many husbands spent too much time bellying up to the bar with the boys. Letitia (whose own husband, it appears, barely touched the stuff) would never question the status quo in terms of roles assigned to men and women—they were God-given, in her book.

So she would never join an organization that used phrases like "women's rights." But temperance was a powerful, and church-supported, movement throughout western Canada. From their pulpits, Protestant churchmen regularly preached about the link between unrestrained boozing and moral depravity.

So temperance was the vehicle for change that traditional women like Letitia were comfortable with. However, that wasn't enough for some members of the WCTU, including Nellie's mother-in-law, Annie McClung. Annie felt that the adoption of temperance by individuals, and the abolition of alcohol by government, was only half the answer: real improvement in women's lives could be won only if women themselves had a say in the way society ran. By the time Nellie had moved from Hazel to Manitou, she had already heard that the preacher's wife had gone round Manitou's parlours, collecting signatures for a petition for women's suffrage. Annie McClung, along with most WCTU leaders, argued that alcohol abuse was part of a general pattern of male disregard for women's needs. The organization recognized that if women had the vote, they could influence legislation and lobby for laws limiting the production and distribution of alcohol. Nellie herself happily signed Annie's petition for women's suffrage, but most of Manitou's respectable matrons had refused to look at such an outrageous document. Nellie would recall later how one of these women ("the wife of the town drunkard") opined that "it's an insult to our husbands to even ask for the vote."

It is easy to laugh at the temperance campaign these days, and the Prohibition zealots with their paraphernalia of white ribbons and abstinence pledge cards. Banning alcohol seems to us about as realistic a goal as banning gas-guzzling SUVs. But in Nellie's day, the prevalence of bars, hotel saloons, and whiskey-selling grocery stores was truly astonishing. Whiskey was cheaper than milk. Moreover, as western historian James H. Gray points out, most of the bars were designed for a single purpose, "stand-up drinking . . . for the purpose of 'getting drunk.'" Old photographs of these bars show dank, low-ceilinged, dirt-floored rooms in which the only stick of furniture is the bar itself: you can almost smell the sour odours of sweat, tobacco, vomit, urine, beer, and whiskey. There was a whole culture of boozing, which included the universal practice of "treating": drinkers regarded the duty to take turns buying a round for everybody present as almost a moral obligation. Add to the availability of alcohol the demographics of Manitoba's pioneer society, in which men far outnumbered women, and the brutally hard work most of them performed, and you have a society characterized by widespread drunkenness.

Nellie McClung would later observe, "It is easy to see why we concentrated on the liquor traffic. It was corporeal and always present; it walked our streets; it threw its challenge in our faces!" She knew of farmers who spent their paltry capital on whiskey rather than seed grain. She saw the local doctor become increasingly incompetent as he took to the bottle. She heard about women whose husbands regularly got roaring drunk and then staggered home to beat them. (She did *not* know any cases of female drinkers. When she finally saw a woman staggering down a Winnipeg street, she was appalled.) As a young teacher in Hazel, she had taught temperance lessons with materials she found in the school cupboard. Her pupils were as mesmerized by their young teacher's fervour as they were by the lurid charts showing the effect of alcohol on the human system: "I think the pictures of inflamed membranes and hob-nailed livers fascinated them."

Nellie was committed to the twin goals of temperance and female suffrage by the time she was in her early twenties. But in the early years of her marriage, she was too busy raising her family, dreaming of becoming a writer, and being an active citizen of Manitou to do much about them. Manitou was the kind of place where a high-energy personality like Nellie was in constant demand. She taught Sunday school; she helped run Christmas concerts, church picnics, Indian club exercises, and community debates; she was a member of the Home Economics Association, a forerunner of the Women's Institute. Her husband was equally busy. Wes McClung was a Mason and also a member of a temperance organization called the Royal Templars; he curled, played lacrosse and hockey, and coached the local boys' baseball team.

The pharmacist and his wife were a fine, upstanding, popular couple, and no Manitou gathering was complete without them. Together they attended all the shows that travelling artists and companies performed at Manitou's community hall. The quality and content of the entertainment was unpredictable, varying from lederhosen-clad Swiss bell-ringers to blackface American spiritual singers, from full-throated bird impersonators to full-chested operatic contraltos. The hall itself was a dusty, drab little place permeated by the smell and smuts of its coal-oil footlights. "But when the blinds were drawn and all the lamps lighted," recalled Nellie, "no opera house that I have ever been in gave out a greater feeling of high expectancy. We dressed in our best for these great occasions. . . . Brides wore their wedding dresses. . . . There were opera wraps which closely resembled piano drapes but no remarks were made. We were too happy to be catty."

For Nellie McClung, these occasions were more than just diversions: they were lessons in stagecraft. One performer in particular captivated her. E. Pauline Johnson, the half-Mohawk, half-English poet from the Six Nations Reserve on Ontario's Grand River, arrived in Manitou and played to capacity crowds in the local Methodist church on two consecutive nights. Pauline Johnson, who had performed in small towns from one end of Canada to the other, knew exactly how to enthrall her audience. Her advertising, Nellie wrote, "had shown only the Indian girl in her beaded chamois costume and feather headdress, so when a beautiful young woman in white satin evening dress came out of the vestry door . . . there was a gasp of surprise from the audience." Nellie and her sister-in-law were so smitten with the diva's lyrical nature poems, followed by fierce verses featuring Indian warriors, that they decided to call on her. "She was the first great personage we had met, and we knew it was a time for white gloves and polished shoes." Nellie decided that Pauline, who also called herself by the Mohawk name Tekahionwake, was "an actress of great power" (although the down-to-earth prairie housewife thought some of the more florid verse lacked "much meaning"). Nellie and Pauline remained in contact until the latter's death in 1913, and Nellie never forgot the onstage spell that Pauline wove, transporting her listeners to "another world, touching the hem of our own romantic past."

Oh, to have such power! Nellie McClung, once the little girl who loved to show off and now a pillar of the community, yearned to create that enchantment herself. Thanks to the WCTU, she had already cut her teeth as a speaker during Saturday afternoon debates. And temperance had once again crept up in her priorities as an issue to be addressed. It was no surprise to Nellie's Manitou friends when she was asked to give the address of welcome at the WCTU's provincial convention, held in her hometown in June 1907. Like an orator in ancient Rome, she knew that presentation was as important as content. "I began my preparations at once," Nellie wrote in the second volume of her memoirs, *The Stream Runs Fast*. "I got a new dress."

I love picturing Nellie striding down the main street of the dusty prairie town toward the town hall that day, with perhaps a hint of nervousness in the way she kept adjusting the angle of the stylish new hat on her curly auburn hair. The hat's red velvet flowers must have accentuated the glow of her cheeks, but I bet the hand that fiddled with the brim was chapped and roughened from gardening, housework, and scrubbing laundry in cold water. It was the first time she would address a sizeable crowd, but she just *knew* she could do it. She was preaching to an all-female audience of the converted, and her easy warmth would establish instant rapport. Most of her listeners would applaud enthusiastically. There were, however, a few who would roll their eyes at her irreverence, and tut-tut at the nerve of the girl. A bit too big for her boots, I can hear them mutter. Too fond of the sound of her own voice. Who does she think she is?

Nellie put her all into that first speech. Alongside the rhetoric of ancient Rome were the instincts of a modern politician. She knew she had to sell a message of hope—"new hopes for a new world," as she put it—rather than give a boring, finger-wagging sermon filled with statistics. "Prohibition is a hard sounding word, worthless as a rallying cry, hard as a locked door or going to bed without your supper." Instead, she painted a picture of the wonderful world that a booze-free future might bring. "Life for both men and women could be made much more attractive with recreation grounds, games, handicrafts, orchestras, folk dances, better houses, better farms." Quaintly folkloric this vision might be—yet in Nellie's enthusiastic rendition, it was magic. Nellie felt her audience responding with the same enthusiasm that Pauline Johnson had triggered after her recital. "I saw faces brighten, eyes glisten, and felt the atmosphere crackle with a new power. I saw what could be done with words. . . . For the first time I knew I had the power of speech."

From that moment, Nellie McClung's talent as a writer would take second place to her flair as a public speaker. She now had two great motivators: her commitment to the temperance cause, and the adrenalin rush of a stage appearance. When *Sowing Seeds in Danny* was published the following year, she had even greater access to the public. Methodist and Presbyterian churches and the local branches of the YMCA or the WCTU in the numerous small towns of Manitoba and Saskatchewan invited Nellie to come and talk to them. Now advertised as an "Elocutionist, Entertainer, and Reader," Nellie McClung was described as like her book, "bright, vivacious and optimistic."

If only some film footage of Nellie in action had survived! "It isn't what she says," commented one fan, "as the way she says it and her wonderful personality." The lessons she had absorbed from Pauline Johnson paid off. One newspaper declared that she was "one of the best entertainments ever held. . . . Every word is heard, every gesture graceful, and her face is full of expression." Nellie was totally at ease onstage. Other than reading from her latest novel, she rarely used a text, and she abhorred the stylized gestures that were the fashion for elocutionists back then. When men speak from a platform, an audience listens first to his words and then, if they like him, looks more carefully at him. But when a woman speaks, as Nellie knew well, the audience decides whether they like how she looks before they hear a word. So Nellie always wore an eye-catching outfit for her performances, and she would make a joke before she embarked on her talk. She would mention her family, and greet old friends, and then, strolling up and down the stage as though moving between cooker and sink, start speaking in the same tone of voice that she used in her own kitchen. She was funny, colloquial, friendly, and—when she had her listeners settled comfortably in their seats—challenging and provocative. And the smile rarely left her face.

E.W. Walker, head of the wholesale department at Toronto's Methodist Book and Publishing House, wrote to her in early 1910: "You must have a regular picnic, a continuous picnic, going to these small burgs being lionized in the way you are, and since you are not the kind who is apt to get a swelled head you must sit back sometimes and revel in it all." Her stage appearances during these years almost always began with readings about the adventures of Pearlie Watson—by 1910, she was giving her listeners a taste of her next Pearlie Watson book, *The Second Chance*. But Nellie rarely left the stage without adding a word about or reading a section of her book dealing with the evils of alcohol. Her outrage about the loneliness and helplessness of many prairie women reinforced the passion with which she spoke. And how she spoke! Her reputation spread eastward, and in late 1910 an Ontario tour was on her schedule, with stops in Whitby, Hamilton, Peterborough, Kingston, Waterloo. In Toronto, where she gave at least five recitals, she "took her audiences by storm." In Port Arthur, on the way home, a local citizen burst into verse to greet her:

> "You have given us Danny, Nellie McClung,
> And Danny has given us you,
> And we clearly trace in his winsome grace,
> The 'Lady of Manitou.'"

Few people realized it at the time, but there was an additional pressure on "the Lady of Manitou" to sell books, besides her eagerness to perform and to improve women's lives. In 1905, Nellie had begun to worry about her husband's mental state. In her published memoirs, she is extremely discreet about the most important relationship in her life, preferring to present herself as the sunny-tempered optimist for whom the clouds are always clearing. Since so few of her private papers have survived, it is not entirely clear what was going on. But in 1905, a shadow fell over the

McClung family: Wes McClung apparently sank into a state
of depression. Nellie ascribed it to his "primitive Methodist
conscience" and "over-cautiousness," which led him to worry
about his pharmacy business. He insisted on checking and
rechecking the prescriptions he had filled, and woke several
times in the night to ensure that the pharmacy was securely
locked. "His usual good disposition began to cloud over,"
Nellie says elliptically. So in December 1905, the McClungs
sold the pharmacy, and with the proceeds bought two farms
that they then rented out. During the next few years, Wes
took a few odd jobs, building telephone lines, for example.
"The years fell away from him," Nellie blithely writes, "and
the whole family was happy."

Was it as simple as that? Wes's neurotic behaviour sounds
suspiciously like an obsessive-compulsive disorder. Up until
this point, he had been a successful professional: his pharmacy
had expanded; he had taken on two assistants and begun to
offer eye examinations and sell glasses. He had built a new
brick building on Manitou's main street, with an upstairs room
where various service clubs held meetings. Now he was the
semi-employed husband of one of Manitou's leading citizens—
a dramatic loss of status within a rigidly conventional and sex-
ist society. The McClungs could rely on the rented farms for
some income, but pressure built on Nellie to be a breadwinner.

Her early short stories paid some of the bills (the *Woman's Home Companion* had paid her five hundred dollars for 20,000 words, and the *Delineator* had paid seventy-five dollars for 2500 words), but freelance earnings were unpredictable. In 1907 she wrote to the editor of the Winnipeg *Telegram*, asking for any kind of writing assignments, such as book reviews. "My reason for wanting such work is because I have to do it and because I need the money. I would be content with a modest remuneration tho, for work of this kind comes easy to me. . . . What I want is a settled sum which will come in every week or month that I can depend on." H. Nicols, the editor, did not oblige. Nellie sent similar pleas to other publications, but from the hints in her journal, it appears that life in Manitou was hand-to-mouth.

With the 1908 publication of *Sowing Seeds in Danny*, the McClungs could enjoy income from Nellie's book sales and speaking engagements. Her 1910 Ontario tour was so lucrative that she returned the following year. (One ladies' organizing committee was so amazed at Nellie's earnings from a Toronto event that they announced they needed a larger share of the proceeds than originally negotiated. Nellie was deeply hurt that they reneged on the deal, then bad-mouthed her as grabby. *They* were not struggling to provide a family income.) As Nellie's fame as an entertainer-recitalist spread, and she travelled more, she must have been reassured to know that Wes was at home, keeping an eye on the household. But in an era when gender roles were rigid and the term "househusband" was still a joke, it must have been hard on Wes. The situation wasn't helped when Nellie's editor, E.S. Caswell, flippantly suggested to Nellie that "a few lessons to 'Wes' in the interval on 'The Care of Children' and 'How to Run a Wifeless Home' would put him in trim for the hiatus in the home" when she visited Ontario.

How Wes felt about this, we don't know. Either he was the saint that Nellie always made him out to be, or he was slowly recovering from a breakdown, or he simply suffered in silence. The strains do not appear to have affected the McClung marriage: throughout Wes's and Nellie's lives, observers always commented on the strength of their bond. When people asked Wes what he thought of his wife's fame, he would say with a quiet smile, "Just call me Mr. Nellie McClung, I don't mind."

Meanwhile, Nellie was outgrowing Manitou and she knew it. She had started to meet other women who shared her interest in both temperance and women's suffrage, and who had the clout to make an impact on these issues. They belonged to the Manitoba branch of the Canadian Women's Press Club— a national organization founded in Toronto in 1904 which had become a magnet for reform-minded women.

The president of the Manitoba CWPC was one of Nellie's first role models: E. Cora Hind, who had also been the first treasurer of the Winnipeg WCTU. A trim little woman with a polite manner and a habit of knitting throughout meetings, Cora was held in awe by both her editors and the city's business community. As agricultural editor of the *Manitoba Free Press*, Cora estimated the size of the harvest each July. In 1904, when eastern Canadian experts had said that there would be only 35 million bushels, because of damage from rust disease, Cora had travelled through the West by train and buggy, checking each field and farm for its potential yield. On her return, she predicted a harvest of 55 million bushels. The crop came in at 54 million bushels: her reputation was made and the fortunes of Winnipeg grain merchants were saved. Now each summer, Cora exchanged her modest woollen skirts for manly breeches and gaiters, donned a big straw hat, and repeated her travels. Bids and prices at the Winnipeg Grain Exchange rose and fell according to Cora Hind's pronouncements. Cora's success had broken down many of the stereotypes about what women could do or write: she did what she was good at, and she did it well.

Cora Hind had visited Manitou in 1892, when eighteen-year-old Nellie was teaching in Hazel. Nellie yearned to introduce herself to "this clever newspaper-woman who was doing with great success the very thing that I aspired to do," but she was too awestruck to step forward. Once Nellie was recognized as an up-and-coming young writer, Cora invited her to be the guest of honour at a CWPC soiree in Winnipeg. On the train from Manitou to Winnipeg, the author of *Sowing Seeds in Danny* stared out at the rolling prairie and wondered anxiously how she would get on with a crowd of city women whose bylines appeared regularly in Winnipeg papers. They were as congenial, she quickly discovered, as the WCTU crowd in Manitou, and while still living in Manitou she managed to attend several subsequent meetings. She relished the chance to talk about how female suffrage would improve the way women were treated.

A few months later, in the fall of 1909, Nellie invited Cora Hind to be her guest in Manitou for a week—a visit that Cora described in an article entitled "The Lady of Manitou" in the *Canadian Home Journal*. The two women got on well, despite the twelve-year age difference. Both were Ontario-born trained teachers (although Cora had never taught, preferring to claim her independence by becoming Winnipeg's first typist, or "typewriter" as they were then called). One morning, Cora and Nellie settled down in the latter's study. In theory, the two women were just going to have an easy time, with Cora on one side of the fireplace, knitting and taking notes, while Nellie dealt with her correspondence and shared her thoughts with her new friend. But Cora counted twenty interruptions—"long distance telephone calls, a visit from the President of the Ladies' Aid, . . . a committee from the Christian Endeavor that wanted advice," plus frequent requests from the McClung children. The way that Nellie handled all the different demands with equanimity, while keeping her husband and children happy, astonished Cora. Nellie was so easy to be with: she was a good listener, but when asked for an opinion or a decision, she didn't hesitate to plunge in. Cora wrote with admiration, "She has, in a pre-eminent degree, that rare virtue, forgetfulness of self and the power to enter the lives and interests of others."

Cora discerned that Nellie McClung would be a wonderful suffrage crusader. With her healthy children, plain-speaking friendliness, and penchant for a well-trimmed hat, she offered beguiling proof that female suffrage and "womanly virtues" were not irreconcilable. Secure within her familial domesticity, she was much more outspoken and cheeky than Cora ever dared to be. Cora's single status and butch breeches made her the target of vicious speculation on her private life—speculation that Nellie would never face. Cora wrote a glowing description of Nellie's household and declared its matriarch "irresistible."

Six years after selling the pharmacy, the McClungs made a dramatic move. In Nellie's careful account, she explains, "One day an insurance man, hearing that Wes had sold his drug store, came out to offer him an agency, and Wes became an agent for the Manufacturers' Life Insurance. In 1911 we moved to Winnipeg, bought a house on Chestnut Street, and the whole tide of life changed."

Nellie implies that she had nothing to do with the move to Winnipeg. Instead, she describes a wistful, tear-filled departure from Manitou. There was a round of farewells, including a dinner at which the town's citizens presented the McClungs with a formal address, which stated that the loss of their illustrious lady author would "leave a void very difficult to fill." As the family travelled to Winnipeg, nostalgia for small-town security surged through Nellie. "Every winding trail seemed like an old friend from whom we were parting. I knew one pleasant chapter of our lives was ending and a sudden fear gripped my heart—fear of the market place; fear of high places; fear of the strange country."

Nellie McClung may have felt stabs of apprehension as the fields of southern Manitoba, already greening with spring wheat, rolled by. But she must have been thrilled to be opening a new chapter in her life. By now, she was an attractive thirty-eight-year-old—waist fashionably corseted with Edwardian rigour, chin as firm as ever, and reputation spreading rapidly. She was a polished public speaker, who had been welcomed as a celebrity in Toronto, where she adopted a new hairstyle with her brown curls swept off her forehead. She knew that a warm welcome awaited her at the cosy, wicker-furnished club room of the CWPC. Most important, her determination to do something about the lack of legal protection for women burned more fiercely than ever. She was eager to crusade for temperance and female suffrage, and she was impatient for social change. Now she too, like her new CWPC friends, would have a chance to make a real impact on the issues that got her fired up. She was definitely ready for high places in the big city.

CHAPTER FIVE

What Works for Women Activists?

Winnipeg, 1911–1914

> I feel that when a man offers hat-lifting when
> we ask for justice we should tell him to keep
> his hat right on. I will go further and say that
> we should tell him not only to keep his hat on
> but to pull it right down over his face.

Winnipeg was the big city—the "bull's eye of the Dominion,"
as its boosters (and there were plenty of them) liked to call it.
The third-largest city in Canada, after Montreal and Toronto,
it had enjoyed spectacular growth over the previous thirty
years. From about 25,000 hardy pioneers in 1880, its population had exploded to 136,035 in 1911—165,000 if you
counted seasonal workers and new arrivals whom the census-
takers had missed. During the previous half century,
Winnipeg had left behind its history as centre of the fur trade
to become the railway capital of Canada, the gateway to the

West, and one of the world's most important hubs for the grain trade. Tall office buildings, encrusted with columns and cornices, had sprung up along Portage Avenue and past the brick bulk of T. Eaton's department store. New streets were spreading west and north, while the tracks of the Canadian Pacific, Canadian Northern, and Grand Trunk railroads fanned out in every direction from the downtown passenger stations, freight yards, slaughterhouses, and meat-packing warehouses.

Winnipeg was also Canada's most multicultural city: Nellie heard German, Polish, Ukrainian, Italian, Russian, and Yiddish spoken on the streets. A majority of Winnipeggers had been born outside Canada, and 25 percent were not "British-born," as the census-takers put it. Even Vancouver, with its large Asian population, didn't top this, while the level of non-Brits in cities like Toronto or Hamilton was as low as 9 percent.

The downside of rapid growth and industrialization was a catalogue of ugly living and working conditions, the likes of which Nellie had rarely seen—overcrowding, badly built tenements, unlicensed sweatshops, inadequate health and school facilities (since school attendance was not compulsory, illiterate kids roamed the streets). Smoke and smuts from steam engines permeated even the finest lace drapes of the millionaires' mansions, with their turrets and *porte cochères*, along Roslyn Road. Men outnumbered women by about ten thousand: crowds of unattached men lurched from bar to bar along Portage and Main. This was not going to be an easy society for women to reform.

The upside of Winnipeg's go-getting buzz was a community far more cultured and cosmopolitan than anything Nellie McClung had ever met before. The city had acquired the grand manner (without, unfortunately, the deep purse) of its American Midwest counterpart, Chicago. In a passage included in an early draft of *The Stream Runs Fast*, Nellie reveals how much she had yearned for the city's attractions while she still lived in Manitou. "When I visited my relatives in Winnipeg, the luxury of hot water, which came to me by the turn of your hand, constituted one of the great pleasures of the visit. I went once a year at least—taking one child with me—and that gave me a lift for the whole year. I saw plays, heard music, and went to the Library." The published version of her memoir does not include this passage, which she probably deemed disloyal to her much-cherished rural roots. Now, she was a resident of Winnipeg, which, unlike the small towns of southwestern Manitoba that she knew, was *not* dominated by transplanted Ontarians, with their prim manners and Protestant pride. Alongside the cacophony of different accents and tongues, there was a far wider range of attitudes and beliefs.

Nellie's first priority, however, was to join forces with the city's cadre of progressive women—"New Women," in the phrase of the day—who were already challenging old-fashioned stereotypes of female behaviour. Throughout the English-speaking world, women were starting to demand the vote, and Winnipeg's New Women were just as interested in the suffrage issue as women in Washington, Toronto, or London. As early as 1848, a women's rights convention had been held in Seneca Falls, New York. In Britain, a bill to grant the vote to women had been introduced in Parliament by the philosopher John Stuart Mill in 1867, but it was defeated by 194 to 73 votes. Since then, British suffragettes like Emmeline Pankhurst and her daughters, Sylvia, Christabel, and Adela, had become increasingly vociferous in their suffrage campaign, staging huge demonstrations and performing headline-grabbing antics such as chaining themselves to London railings.

Alongside Cora Hind, Winnipeg's most radical activists included Kate Simpson Hayes, Kennethe Haig, and Francis Beynon and her sister Lillian Beynon Thomas. These were women whose articles were regularly published in newspapers, and who had the power to sway public opinion. By 1911, the Winnipeg CWPC boasted thirty-one members. The close-knit "Press Clubbers" met regularly to discuss writing and reform, drew strength from one another, and offered support to "any woman who is doing something for the uplift of the sex." But support for female suffrage within Manitoba was still unfocused. Activists still had not developed a strategy for a suffrage campaign, although they could see the link between the suffrage issue and the larger challenge of urban reform.

THE MCCLUNG FAMILY spent the first two months after their departure from Manitou at a cottage at Matlock Beach, on Lake Winnipeg. In the fall, they moved into 97 Chestnut Street, a rambling three-story clapboard house in Winnipeg's elm-lined Wolseley district, a short walk west of the legislative building. The McClung's Winnipeg home was typical of all the McClung homes in subsequent years: a foreign-born maid kept the kitchen spotless, children's sports equipment littered the front hall, and the parlour was always ready to welcome surprise visitors and delegations. In 1911, Mark, the last member of the family, was born. In Nellie's memoirs, she mentions Mark's birth almost as an aside before going on to discuss the most important routine of her new life in Winnipeg: the weekly teas of the CWPC's Winnipeg branch. "It was not enough for us to meet and talk and eat chicken sandwiches and olives. We felt we should organize and create a public sentiment in favour of women's suffrage."

Influenced by her new friends, Nellie McClung broadened her perspective on how to improve women's lives. She continued to argue for the kind of reforms that were priorities for rural women: legislation that would give women rights to marital property and to guardianship of their children, and also an amendment to the Homestead Act to permit women, like men, to be granted free land. But now she learned for the first time about the desperate lives of poor immigrant women in the city: "we were greatly stirred over the question of long hours, small wages and distressing working conditions." She still believed that alcohol was the root of most social problems, but Winnipeg showed her how little legal protection was available for women domestics and factory workers. She got involved through the Methodist Church with a man who would reshape the political landscape of Canada in subsequent decades—James Shaver Woodsworth. Woodsworth had founded the All People's Mission to help Eastern European immigrants in the city's North End learn the language and customs of their new country, and to provide their children with education and recreation. Nellie visited rundown homes and saw hungry, barefoot children. She watched women in filthy basement workshops struggling to fill sewing quotas while their children were left in squalid, overcrowded tenements under the care of older siblings.

Since the end of the previous century, women's organizations had pressed the province's Conservative government
for stricter control of liquor sales, stronger enforcement of
factory safety laws, and legal protection for widows, but
their petitions had been brushed aside. Once settled in
Chestnut Street, Nellie threw herself into these issues. At
one of the first meetings of the Local Council of Women
that she attended, she heard Mrs. Claude Nash speak about
the plight of women working in factories. Nellie was horrified. Within a couple of days, she and Mrs. Nash had decided to visit the Conservative premier to recommend that he
appoint a woman factory inspector. The encounter would
prove historic—Nellie's clashes with Sir Rodmond Roblin
made her reputation, and have become part of the mytholo-
gy of Manitoba, Canada, and women's history.

Premier Roblin was a vigorous and able politician, a man
"of great energy, simplicity and directness of mind" in the
words of the Manitoba historian W.L. Morton. He had a
broad tolerance of differing views (he was one of the few
Protestant, English-speaking legislators who had supported
the right of French-speaking Manitobans to separate schools)
and a vigilant realism in reading both public opinion and
partisan interests. He supported Prohibition in theory; in
practice, he was evasive because he didn't want to alienate

either liquor producers or Roman Catholic voters who didn't take to the idea of temperance. He had made a fortune in the grain trade, and his shrewdness had kept him in office for the past eleven years. Before Nellie's arrival, he looked set for at least another decade in the premier's chair.

But Sir Rodmond Roblin was, in Nellie's phrase, "a gentleman of the old school." He had no idea how to deal with New Women and their extraordinary assumption that they should be more than handmaidens to their menfolk. When Nellie and Mrs. Nash appeared in his office, he was dazzled by these two attractive and well-dressed women and "expressed his delight at our coming." He was taken aback when they suggested he should accompany them on a tour of factories, but reluctantly agreed. "He called his car and we set out," recounted Nellie. "He looked very well in his beaver coat, and his car was the most pretentious I had ever ridden in. The cut glass vase filled with real carnations impressed my country eyes."

Nellie had such fun writing her account of this jaunt with the premier that I am almost tempted to feel sorry for the old relic, who appeared to think he was out for a spin with two Gibson girls. "On the way to the first factory, the Premier, who sat between us with his plump hands resting on a gold-headed cane, gave us his view on women working in factories. He believed in work, especially for young women. There was too much idleness now, with electricity and short cuts in labour. . . . And these young girls in the factories whom we thought were underpaid, no doubt they lived at home, and really worked because they wanted pin-money. Anyway, working wouldn't hurt them, it would keep them off the streets. . . . Most of the women in the factories, he understood, were from foreign countries, where life was strenuous. . . . It doesn't do women any harm to learn how money comes."

The factories they visited were nightmares. The premier found himself in airless basements with no ventilation, no heat, and refuse all over the floors. In one, conversation was drowned out by the noise of the machinery and the only toilet was backed up. In the second, one worker was obviously injured and another sick. Sir Rodmond staggered into the open air, then turned to his companions and said, "I still can't see why two women like you should ferret out such utterly disgusting things."

Nellie McClung learned some important lessons from this excursion with the premier. She recognized that this gentleman of the old school had little real interest in social reforms: he would move only under pressure. She realized he was a delicious subject for mockery, her weapon of choice when trying to undermine an opponent's arguments. And she, along with a core of other activist women, decided that lobbying for stronger legislation or regulation of factories was never going to be enough: they should go for the vote. The Local Council of Women could not be the vehicle for a suffrage campaign because, although its members hooted with laughter at Nellie's description of her jaunt with the premier, many of them, she noted, had husbands "who would not let them 'go active.' It might imperil their jobs." Instead, a group of about fifteen female suffrage campaigners and liberal-minded men formed the Political Equality League, with the expressed goal of female suffrage in Manitoba.

"Votes for Women" campaigns were erupting elsewhere in Canada. Since 1898, the provinces rather than the federal government controlled suffrage eligibility, so Canadian suffragettes made provincial governments the focus of their efforts, particularly in Ontario, British Columbia, and Manitoba. In March 1909, a delegation of over four hundred men and women presented Sir James Whitney, the Ontario premier, with a petition said to contain one hundred thousand signatures, demanding votes for women. "Crush of Women Seek Votes," blared the headline in the *Evening Telegram*: "Sir James says 'Not Now.'" In June that year, Toronto hosted the fourth annual meeting of the International Council of Women. Within Canada, suffrage activists were split between two rival organizations: the Canadian Suffrage Association and the National Union of Women Suffrage Societies of Canada. The latter organization claimed Nellie McClung as a convenor, but Nellie paid little attention to the national picture.

However, all the Winnipeg Press Clubbers watched with interest the militant tactics employed by British suffragettes. Fuelled by frustration with the Westminster government's failure to legislate women's suffrage, the Pankhursts and their allies had ratcheted up their campaign to include bombs and arson. One activist threw a hatchet at Liberal prime minister Asquith; acid was poured into mailboxes. Within five days, 124 women were arrested: many promptly embarked on headline-catching hunger strikes. Manitoba's Political Equality League had no interest in the aggressively confrontational style adopted by the Pankhursts (one of the British slogans was "Votes for Women, Chastity for Men"). Violence, in the words of Lillian Beynon Thomas, should be "the tactic of last resort." However, when Emmeline Pankhurst visited Winnipeg, Nellie entertained her at 97 Chestnut Street. Nellie had no time for lawlessness, but she warmed to the fiery militant. "I would rather take my place with [her] in the last day than with the women who sit at home babbling of indirect influence and womanly charm but never doing anything for the betterment of humanity."

There was no bomb throwing in Winnipeg. Instead, there was a dogged campaign to build public support through hard work and strategic alliances. Petitions were circulated, gathering hundreds of signatures. One hundred suffrage banners were printed to adorn Winnipeg streetcars. Nellie insisted on adding a "Votes for Women" message to every Pearlie Watson speech she gave—and she was busier on the speaking circuit than ever. Cora Hind and Francis Beynon promoted in their *Free Press* columns both the league and the pamphlets it published, including *The Legal Status of Women in Manitoba* by Dr. Mary Crawford and *The New Citizenship* by Nellie L. McClung.

Although these westerners got less press than their Toronto counterparts, they enjoyed more backing from both rural women and progressive men. Across the prairies, where life was so hard in those days, there was a powerful sense of collectivity, which meant that everyone—even someone advocating such dangerous notions as feminism—was part of the community. There was also a persistent streak of radicalism, which in time would spawn the United Farmers, the Co-operative Commonwealth Federation, and the Social Credit movement. So the Political Equality League had the official endorsement of powerful farm organizations as well as the support of the *Manitoba Free Press* and the weekly *Grain Growers' Guide*, the official voice of the Grain Growers' Association of Manitoba and Saskatchewan, and the United Farmers of Alberta. George Chipman, editor of the *Grain Growers' Guide*, wrote so many pro-suffrage editorials that in 1913 he received a letter from an irate Saskatchewan farmer threatening to cancel his subscription if the editorials didn't stop. "My wife gets the *Guide*," he wrote, "and reads your articles to me at the supper table and it makes things very unpleasant in my home." (The editorials never stopped, but the subscription was never cancelled.) The provincial Liberal Party, under the leadership of the genial T.C. Norris, was considering a promise of female suffrage for its election platform. Meanwhile, with dangerous complacency, Conservative premier Roblin sneered that suffrage was supported only by "short-haired women and long-haired men."

The league also turned to a favourite weapon of Canadian suffragettes—the "mock parliament." As early as 1883, Amelia Yeomans, a leading light of the Manitoba WCTU, had starred in a mock parliament held in Winnipeg. Mrs. Yeomans had acted the part of the premier, and an all-women cast of legislators had debated whether men should be given the vote.

Similar mock parliaments had been held in Vancouver and Toronto, to build support and raise funds. Now Winnipeg campaigners had a powerful new weapon—the most popular speaker in the province. Nellie had also demonstrated her sheer nerve. On an impulse, she had called on the premier again to make the case for women's suffrage. Sir Rodmond Roblin listened with "amused tolerance" as she explained why he should be taking the issue of women's suffrage seriously. As Nellie gleefully recorded in her memoirs, he gave the following reply: "Why do women want to mix in the hurly-burly of politics? My mother was the best woman in the world, and she certainly never wanted to vote! I respect women. I honor and reverence women, I lift my hat when I meet a woman. . . . Take it from me, nice women don't want the vote."

Nellie chortled as "his voice dripped fatness." The meeting gave her the chance to size up her opponent in the fight, and to gather material for her speeches on the suffrage issue. "By nice women . . . you probably mean selfish women who have no more thought for the underpaid, overworked women than a pussy cat in a sunny window has for the starving kitten on the street," she told the premier. "Now in that sense I am not a nice woman, for I do care. I care about those factory women, working in ill-smelling holes, and we intend to do something about it, and when I say 'we' I'm talking for a great many women, of whom you will hear more as the days go by." Sir Rodmond gave a condescending, dismissive smile. What a mistake! As soon as Nellie was out of the door, she had shaped the meeting into a hilarious anecdote starring the premier as an old fool. Her audiences applauded wildly.

The stage was set. In January 1914, while Nellie was on a speaking tour outside Winnipeg, her league colleagues decided they would send a delegation to the legislature to make their first formal request for voting rights for women. At the same time, they booked the city's Walker Theatre for their own mock parliament the day after the meeting. When Nellie returned to Winnipeg, she was told that she was to play the part of Sir Rodmond Roblin.

The delegation that met in front of the legislature on January 27, 1914, drew from a far wider spectrum of humanity than any suffrage demonstration in Toronto or Britain. There were broad-faced women in headscarves from the First Icelandic Women's Suffrage Association (founded in the 1890s, it was the oldest suffrage organization in the West), and wool-coated women from the WCTU, the Women's Civic League, and the Mothers' Association. There were ruddy-faced farmers from the Manitoba Grain Growers' Association, and tobacco-chewing labourers from the Trades and Labour Council. There were shabby factory workers and beefy bus conductors. "It represented many nationalities," according to the highly sympathetic report in the *Grain Growers' Guide*, "Anglo-Saxon, Icelandic, Hebrew, African, Polish. . . . High-browed professors were there shoulder to shoulder with plain working girls. Nurses, lawyers, business-men, journalists, doctors and quiet little housewives whom the census describes as having no occupation. . . . It filled the legislative chamber and overflowed into the gallery and from the ladies' gallery into the press gallery."

As one of the main spokespeople, Nellie McClung was seated at a table within the chamber. She laid out the argu-ments why women should have the vote. She anticipated the objection that politics was too corrupt a sphere for women. The *Grain Growers' Guide* reported her speech: "There is nothing inherently vicious about politics, and the politi-cian who says politics are corrupt is admitting one of two things—that he is party to that corruption or that he is unable to prevent it. In either case we take it that he is flying the white signal of distress and we are willing and even anx-ious to come over and help him. (Applause and laughter)."

Sir Rodmond Roblin replied in his usual tone of supercil-ious amusement. He suggested that if female suffrage was inevitable, it would come in its own good time. But look around! All the campaign had achieved in England, thanks to those militant Pankhursts and their friends, was "such hysteria as to endanger human life and result in destruction of millions of dollars worth of property." And after women started voting in the United States, the fabric of family life had crumbled. "For every marriage in the United States, there is a divorce," he suggested, without a fact to support him. "Will you tell me that that is in the interests of society?"

Nellie McClung smiled sweetly as Sir Rodmond spoke. Had the premier offered any concessions, "he could have pricked our beautiful balloon." Instead, he puffed on—and she listened carefully. "He was making the speech that I would make in the play in less than thirty-six hours." She memorized not only his words, but also his gestures and every tone of voice, "from the ingratiating friendly voice . . . to the loud masterful commanding voice which brooked no opposition." Then she rushed home and practised it all in front of the mirror—sticking her thumbs into the armholes of her jacket, wagging her head, and teetering on her heels.

The following night in the packed Walker Theatre, when the house lights dimmed and the curtain rose, a cast of female legislators, their evening dresses cloaked in black robes, was revealed. It was pure Theatre of the Absurd. Various male petitioners stepped onstage to request attention to such diverse matters as the need for modesty in male clothing (decent men should not wear scarlet ties or squeaky shoes), and the necessity of a ban on alkali in laundry soap as it ruined men's delicate hands. The audience, mainly female but including several Conservative and Liberal men, roared with laughter.

Finally, a delegation arrived with a wheelbarrow of petitions, all requesting votes for men. As Nellie took centre stage, a rustle of delight and anticipation swept through the audience. With perfect timing, Nellie raised her chin, paused—and then let rip. In a brilliant impersonation of Premier Roblin's manner, she congratulated the delegates on their good looks, but then shook her head sadly. If all men were as intelligent as this misguided delegation, the government might consider the request. But they were not. According to Nellie's own handwritten draft for the speech, "the premier" went on to say, "Seven-eighths of the police court offenders are men, and only one-third of church membership. You ask me to enfranchise these? . . . O no, man is made for something higher and better than voting. Men were made to support families. What is home without a bank account? The man who pays the grocer rules the world." Wagging her head and rocking backwards on her heels, Nellie continued to mimic Roblin's patronizing manner. "In this agricultural province, the man's place is the farm. Shall I call man away from the useful plow and harrow to talk loud on street corners about things that do not concern him? Politics unsettle men, and unsettled men means unsettled bills—broken furniture and broken vows—and divorce. . . . When you ask for the vote you are asking me to break up peaceful, happy homes—to wreck innocent lives."

The event, in the words of the *Winnipeg Tribune*, was the "best burlesque ever staged in Winnipeg . . . smiles of anticipation, ripples of merriment, gales of laughter and storms of applause punctuated every point and paragraph." Even the *Winnipeg Telegram*, a Conservative newspaper, described Nellie McClung's speech as "the choicest piece of sarcasm that has ever been heard locally. . . . It was somewhat overdone, perhaps, but for the purposes of the entertainment, it was entirely suitable." The Political Equality League's mock parliament was so successful that it was repeated a few days later in Winnipeg and then staged in Brandon. Nellie McClung's reputation as an attractive and witty standard-bearer for the suffrage campaign was sealed. Nellie herself was so proud of her efforts that she included the whole episode in *Purple Springs*, the third volume of her fictional Pearlie Watson trilogy, putting into Pearlie's mouth the speech she herself had given.

Euphoria swept the Manitoba suffragists. Overnight, suffrage had become respectable and fashionable: the momentum of their movement seemed unstoppable. The provincial Liberal Party invited the Political Equality League to address its annual convention. Nellie's speech triggered rousing cheers from the predominantly male audience. Scenting a vote-winner, the party resolved to introduce both temperance and women's suffrage if the Liberals formed the government after the coming election. Nellie stumped the province in support of these two Liberal promises, becoming politically partisan for the first time in her life. In one week, she packed the local hall in Minto on Monday, Elgin on Tuesday, Melita on Wednesday, and Killarney on Thursday. She often arrived in a town immediately after the premier had spoken. With tongue in cheek and thumbs thrust into an imaginary vest's armholes, she would send him up and mock his promises to tighten up liquor controls. When Roblin complained that he was being made to appear anti-Prohibition, when all he was doing was opposing the idea of a referendum on the subject, Nellie went for the jugular. "His halo of being a temperance man seems to be in danger of slipping, and he is holding it with both hands while trying to pat himself on the back with another. It is an unnatural position."

Other women, including Lillian Beynon Thomas and Francis Beynon, campaigned in 1914, but in an age when political oratory was one of the few forms of entertainment available, Nellie McClung outshone everyone else. Manitoba voters not only flocked to Nellie's political rallies: they even paid an entrance fee. Both fans and critics loved her attacks on members of the legislature, politicians then as now being sitting ducks for comedy. One of Nellie's favourite anecdotes concerned the Conservative member who had not spoken for years. People in the gallery began to wonder whether he was alive. Then a draft from an open window made him sneeze one day, and he rose to close the window. This, announced a triumphant Nellie, was the only initiative he had ever taken all by himself!

Along with Nellie's repertoire of cheeky stories was her skill at repartee. Critics quickly learned not to make themselves the butt of her jokes. One man listened to her explaining the benefits of having female suffrage, then called out, "In Colorado, where women vote, a woman once stuffed a ballot box [with counterfeit votes]. How can the lady explain that?" McClung shot back: "No one could expect women to live all their lives with men without picking up some of their little ways!"

Nellie McClung not only took on her opponents' argument that women were "too good" for the hurly-burly of politics. She also confronted the racism implicit in the Conservative suggestion that female suffrage was unthinkable because it would allow "ignorant" immigrant women to vote. Nellie would have none of this: women should receive the franchise on the same basis as men. "In our blind egotism we class our foreign people as ignorant people, if they do not know our ways and our language. They may know many other languages, but if they have not yet mastered ours they are poor ignorant foreigners. We Anglo-Saxon people have a decided sense of our own superiority. . . . We have no reason to be afraid of the foreign woman's vote. I wish we were as sure of the ladies who live on the Avenue."

During the 1914 campaign, Nellie's speeches were roundly applauded by Liberal crowds and newspapers, and condemned by Conservative supporters and press. Once onstage, she revelled in her success. Backstage, however, she found herself dealing with a more hurtful political weapon—whisper campaigns. She had left her five children in the care of her husband and two domestic helpers, and she checked regularly that the household on Chestnut Street was running smoothly. She began her speeches with a cheerful reassurance that she had just phoned home and her children were fine. But rumours swirled that her children were neglected and running wild, and her husband contemplating divorce. "That is the one part of my public life that has really hurt," she would later write. "There are people mean enough to show hostility and spite to the children. . . . It is all rather pitiful to know that people can be that cruel."

Her family got used to reading about their mother's speeches in the papers: accounts in the *Winnipeg Tribune* and the *Manitoba Free Press* were always admiring, since these were Liberal papers, whereas the pro-Roblin *Winnipeg Telegram* dismissed her as "windy Nellie." The children quickly smartened up to public life. One day Horace found a mud-spattered Mark wrestling with another youngster. He grabbed him by his shirt collar and marched him down the back lane into the McClung yard through a hole in the fence. "Quick now!" he told his younger brother, according to Nellie's memoirs. "It's a good thing I got you before the *Telegram* got a picture of you —Nellie McClung's neglected child!"

Despite malicious rumours and campaign fatigue, this must have been one of the happiest periods in Nellie's life. Wes was doing fine in his job; her children were well cared for, and still too young to cause any concerns; she herself was surrounded by friends and at the top of her game. Newspapers from as far away as Quebec followed her exploits. "Manitoba Tories Worried over Lady Orator's Campaign," read the *Montreal Herald* headline on July 9, 1914. "Thousands flock to hear her address." How *satisfying*. Her self-esteem and book sales soared. She was known nationally as "Our Nell."

Despite everything, Roblin's Conservatives enjoyed their fifth straight win in the July 1914 election. The election had been "a contest between the past and the future," in the words of historian W.L. Morton, "and the past was strong and deeply entrenched."

But the 1914 election was a watershed, and the future beckoned. The Conservative majority was reduced, and the election re-established Norris's Liberals as a credible government-in-waiting. Less than a year later, Sir Rodmond was forced to resign, after his government was accused of corruption in the awarding of contracts for the new legislative building. The Liberals won a landslide victory in August 1915, and in January 1916 they honoured their election pledge. The women of Manitoba became the first Canadian women to win the right to vote in provincial elections and to hold provincial office. Five months later, the Manitoba Temperance Act, which in effect banned the sale of liquor anywhere in the province, became law. The future had arrived.

Would the Political Equality League have achieved this goal without Nellie McClung? Probably, but I think it might have taken a few more years. The campaign was well launched by the time she arrived in Winnipeg, and other suffragists played crucial roles. But there is no doubt that in 1914 Nellie had established a national reputation as a formidable political fighter, and in this campaign she discovered a winning combination of tenacious purpose and role-reversal humour. Angry martyrdom had been the weapon of choice for British suffragettes. In Canada, what worked for women was solidarity and Nellie's trademark satire.

By the time women in Manitoba won the vote, however, Nellie's family and attention were elsewhere.

CHAPTER SIX

What Do Women Want?

Edmonton, 1914–1919

> I cannot help but think that if there had been
> women in the German Reichstag, women with
> authority behind them, when the Kaiser began
> to lay his plans for the war, the results might
> have been very different. I do not believe
> women with boys of their own would ever sit
> down and willfully plan slaughter, and if there
> had been women there when the Kaiser and
> his brutal warlords discussed the way in which
> they would plunge all Europe into bloodshed,
> I believe one of those deep-bosomed, motherly,
> blue-eyed German women would have stood upon
> her feet and said, "William—forget it!"

Nellie McClung's breezy self-assurance and Methodist zeal faltered in the next few years. Winning the vote had been a straightforward objective; now she faced less clearcut issues that often sparked disagreements within her circle. Once women had the vote, they had to decide how to use it. What did they *want*?

Divisions emerged even before women in Manitoba had finally won the vote. Events had moved quickly for Nellie after the July 1914 election campaign. The McClungs retreated to their Matlock Beach cottage on Lake Winnipeg for the summer. Children splashed in the water and played on the sand while adults spent long lazy afternoons on the porch. Nellie relaxed after the intensity of the political campaign, and enjoyed watching the lake ripple in the sun. When she felt an urge for activity, she kneaded dough and baked bread. But on August 3, the small cottage community was stunned to hear that, thousands of kilometres away, Great Britain ("the mother country" for many cottagers) had declared war on Germany. Few people had heard of the Austro-Hungarian grand duke whose assassination in June had triggered the declaration; even fewer understood what this meant for Manitoba. "Couldn't we let them fight out their own battles?" Nellie, along with others, wondered. But the outbreak of a distant war put an end to dreamy bread making. Within three weeks, the McClungs had packed up their cottage and returned to Winnipeg.

The first shock for Nellie was the discovery that the Press Clubbers were divided in their attitude to war. Her friend and mentor Cora Hind was adamant that Britain's battles were also Canada's. "We were British and must follow the tradition of our fathers." But Francis Beynon and her sister Lillian Beynon

Thomas were resolute pacifists. So was J.S. Woodsworth, who ran the All People's mission in Winnipeg's North End and with whose progressive social views Nellie felt at home. Nellie deplored Cora's fiery denunciations of anybody who disagreed with her, but felt torn between old friends. She grappled with her own ambivalence as she watched troop trains pull out of Winnipeg's station and mothers weep as they waved goodbye to husbands and sons. The debate over Canada's role loosened the bonds between those who had fought the good fight for women's suffrage.

Most difficult for Nellie was a new development in her husband's career. Wes's health problems appeared to be behind him and he was doing well at the Manufacturers' Life Insurance Company—so well, in fact, that the company had offered him a promotion to manager of either its Edmonton or Vancouver branch. Nellie would have to abandon the province in which she had lived since childhood, and the city where she had made such good friends. She was a star in Manitoba, and although she was never an egotist, there's no doubt that she enjoyed public recognition. She had even started to muse about the possibility, once women had the vote, of getting elected in Manitoba and serving in a Liberal government. Now she would have to start again in completely unfamiliar surroundings.

In her memoirs, chin-up Nellie made the best of it: "We decided on Edmonton . . . we believed that Alberta, with its mines, prairies and mountains, its newness, its incoming settlers would suit us. . . . I would get a chance to go back to my writing in a new province. . . . I would shed my political alliances, and go back to the work I liked best." But for an activist, who had thrown herself with gleeful gusto into Manitoba's political maelstrom, such a scenario was not just unlikely—it was willful self-deception. Edmonton was a quarter the size of Winnipeg, with nothing like the buzz and bustle of "the Chicago of the North." It wasn't even on the CPR's transcontinental rail line. Nevertheless, in December 1914, Nellie packed up her household, waved a tearful goodbye to the comfortable home on Chestnut Street, and along with her five children, Irish housekeeper, and dog boarded the westbound train. The members of the Political Equality League presented her with a farewell address, in which they described her as "the universal woman, who cannot be localized" and said that it was "only fair that they should share her with another province."

AS SOON AS THE MCCLUNGS WERE SETTLED in their new home on Edmonton's 123rd Street, Nellie did concentrate on writing. With her usual self-discipline, she went to her desk each morning after her four eldest children had gone to school, and turned out a thousand words a day. Within a matter of weeks, she had produced several short stories and *In Times Like These*, her fourth book. This book, which appeared in 1915 and has always remained in print, is recognized today as the most important Canadian statement of what we now call first-wave feminism.

In Times Like These demonstrated Nellie McClung's strengths as a writer and orator. Based on various lectures she had given to political and church groups, it captured her talent for polemic and was spiced with acerbic wit and down-to-earth common sense. Its sections had catchy titles like "What Do Women Think of War? (Not that It Matters)." It included some of McClung's poetry, such as the "Anti-Suffrage Creed":

> I hold it true—I will not change,
> For changes are a dreadful bore—
> That nothing must be done on earth
> Unless it has been done before.

However, it also revealed a strand in her pre-1914 belief system that seems hopelessly naïve today: her conviction that women are morally superior to men.

In the Manitoba suffrage campaign, this faith in women's power for good had been one of the grounds on which Nellie and her comrades (all white, middle class, and English speaking) had demanded the vote. In common with most women of the period, including unmarried women, they identified motherhood as women's crucial role within society, and they argued that if women could have some input into the legislative system, they could bring valuable maternal instincts to bear on social problems. A bloc of female votes, went the argument, would go some way to controlling the forces that threatened family life, because women pay more attention to social needs than material gain. Education, civic cleanliness, reform of delinquent children, infant mortality, public health, child labour—suffragists argued that these were all appropriate issues for women to have a say on. Canada was changing. With rapid industrialization, the home was a beleaguered fortress against alcohol, crime, disease, and all the other forces of immorality that stalked city streets. "A re-invigorated motherhood, the natural occupation for virtually all women," as historian Veronica Strong-Boag describes their reasoning, "could serve as a buttress against all the destabilizing elements in Canada. . . . Vote in hand, [women] would be able to maximize their influence for good." Such an argument was comfortably unthreatening for early twentieth-century Canadians. It made the Votes for Women campaign seem little more than a plea for women to extend their traditional housekeeping duties.

Now, in her first nonfiction book, Nellie expanded this "maternal feminist" argument. In the essay "What Do Women Think of War? (Not that It Matters)," she stated baldly, "Women are naturally the guardians of the race." Women wanted peace. However, women themselves must show some initiative, especially now that political influence was within their grasp. The author had no time for women who hid behind their husband's name or conventional wisdom, wallowed in "cow-like contentment," and didn't think for themselves. In the astringent essay "Should Women Think?" she wrote, "The most deadly uninteresting person, and the one who has the greatest temptation not to think at all, is the comfortable and happily married woman—the woman who has a good man between her and the world, who has not the saving privilege of having to work. A sort of fatty degeneration of the conscience sets in that is disastrous to the development of thought." Women must participate in public life, and make legislators pay attention to their priorities. Once on the warpath against "parasitism," there was nothing Nellie wouldn't poke fun at. In an essay entitled sarcastically "Gentle Lady," she targeted attitudes and fashions that hobbled women's capacities. "The hideous mincing gait of the tightly-skirted women seems to speak. It [says]: I am not a useful human being—see, I cannot walk, I dare not run."

The maternal feminist argument predominated in *In Times Like These*, but Nellie also came out swinging in a broader defence of human rights. She believed that true democracy would be achieved only if every adult, regardless of gender, had the right to participate in government. "The time will come, we hope," she wrote, "when women will be economically free, and mentally and spiritually independent enough to refuse to have their food paid for by men; when women will receive equal pay for equal work and have all avenues of activity open to them; and will be free to choose their own mates, without shame or indelicacy. . . . The new movement among women who are crying out for a larger humanity is going to bring it about." This was a much more radical challenge to the status quo, since it assumed that women were the equals of men rather than a subspecies of the human race. Flora MacDonald Denison, a columnist for the *Toronto Sunday World* and for *Saturday Night* who was prominent in the Ontario-based Canadian Suffrage Association, made the same point even more bluntly: "Labour is not defined by gender and washing dishes is no more feminine than the sending of a marconigram [an early form of telegram] is masculine."

The times that Nellie analyzed in *In Times Like These* were times of war. In 1915, Nellie's position on the

European hostilities was that war was an unmitigated evil, perpetrated by men and motivated by "the withering, blighting, wasting malady of hatred, which has its roots in the narrow patriotism which teaches people to love their own country and despise all others." She even argued that war sapped the national gene pool, because the fittest went to fight, and "the epileptic, the consumptive, the inebriate . . . stay at home and perpetuate the race." If women had been in charge, war would never have been declared and the German army would never have overrun Belgium. German women should have protested their kaiser's dictum that "women have only two concerns in life, cooking and children" and demanded a role in public affairs. Because they didn't, their sons had marched through Belgium, "leaving behind them smoking trails of ruin, black as their own hard hearts!"

However, this argument didn't answer the question of how Canada should respond to German aggression: Nellie was still torn on that issue. Her insistence that if women ruled the world, war would never have broken out triggered ridicule at the time. A *Saturday Night* reviewer called it "hysterical and fantastic bunkum." (It looks even wackier today, after subsequent experience with leaders like Indira Gandhi, Golda Meir, and Margaret Thatcher.)

Nellie did take the opportunity, in her book, to promote the idea of Canada as the land of the future. Each morning at the breakfast table she would read aloud with shock the news reports of devastation and hunger in Europe, and compare the misery there with Canada's fertile, empty acres waiting for settlers. "The prairie, with its peace and silence, calls to the troubled nations of Middle Europe, where people are caught in the cruel tangle of war." She suggested that Canada, which she characterized as "the land of the Fair Deal" or "the Second Chance," offered European survivors the opportunity to start their lives afresh, in a society where "every race, colour and creed will be given exactly the same chance." This was a highly romanticized portrayal of a country where anti-Semitism was widespread, Aboriginal peoples were excluded from their traditional lands, theatres and swimming pools in most cities banned Asians and blacks, and Chinese immigrants were obliged to pay a fifty-dollar head tax. However, Nellie's rosy vision reflected the spirit of a new social movement to which she, along with her friends the Beynon sisters, was strongly attracted: the Social Gospel movement.

Deeply rooted in the Methodism that Nellie herself held so dear, the Social Gospel movement, founded by her old Winnipeg friend J.S. Woodsworth, was an attempt to apply

Christian principles to the urban problems that so concerned the suffrage leaders. Its goals overlapped with many of those of early feminists: community action, Prohibition, expansion of welfare programs, development of co-operatives. Woodsworth wrote extensively on the need to establish the kingdom of heaven in the "here and now." The ideas of Woodsworth and other activists, including Tommy C. Douglas, would transform the politics of the Prairie provinces in the years to come in directions with which Nellie was in complete agreement. But Nellie could never bring herself to embrace the Social Gospellers' pacifism during the First World War, or their increasing radicalism afterwards. So throughout *In Times Like These*, the author ducked the whole question of Canada's continuing involvement in European hostilities. Instead, she concentrated on urging women to assert themselves and improve society.

But the McClung family could not keep the war at arm's length forever. Nellie was horrified by tales of German atrocities in Belgium (some of which turned out to be British propaganda). Her outrage was reinforced in May 1915, with news that a German U-boat had sunk the *Lusitania*, a passenger ship, just off the Irish coast, killing 1,198 of the 1,962 people aboard. "Then I saw," she wrote, "that we were waging war on the very Princes of Darkness. . . . I knew then that no man could die better than in defending civilization from this ghastly thing which threatened her!"

Subconsciously, she was preparing herself for the moment that she dreaded: the moment when her eldest son would come swinging through the front door of the McClung residence and announce he had signed up. Jack, who had inherited his father's gentle smile and his mother's strong will, was now a strapping eighteen-year-old. He was also a particular comfort to his mother. He could make her laugh: he "always seemed to read my mind, [and] knew when I was feeling low." Sure enough, Jack enlisted. The whole family accompanied him to the railway station early in the morning of December 4, 1915, as he took the train east. Nellie refused to cry as she waved goodbye, but it was a "squeamish, sickly, choky time."

With Jack's departure, Nellie, now forty-two, realized that her own youth was over. Whatever her critics might suggest, she loved being a mother, and she felt her own life diminished as her family grew up and started to leave. Although she was never one to express much self-doubt, she must have asked herself, should she have travelled less, and played a larger role in raising her children instead of leaving them to Wes and her domestic helpers? On her return from the station, she gathered up Jack's schoolbooks, notes, and baseball mitt and carried them to the attic storeroom. There, surrounded by boxes of old clothes and forgotten toys, and out of sight of the rest of the family, she sat down and howled with grief and fear. Until the guns fell silent, supplications on Jack's behalf figured prominently in the family's evening prayers. Anxiety about her firstborn would be a constant companion for Nellie McClung—and would shape her responses to the war.

EDMONTON MIGHT HAVE BEEN SMALLER than Winnipeg during these years, with a population of only fifty thousand (the population of the whole of Alberta was less than four hundred thousand), but it had a similar gang of women activists who welcomed the arrival of Nellie McClung. Representatives from the Edmonton Equal Franchise League, the Edmonton Women's Press Club, the local branch of the Women's Christian Temperance Union, and the Edmonton Women's Missionary Society lined up to call on the famous author. Despite Nellie's insistence that she wanted to focus on books now, she would always greet them with a welcoming smile and invite them in for a chat. Soon Nellie had a new circle of friends and a familiar battle—the suffrage battle in Alberta. Within weeks of her arrival in Edmonton, and while *In Times Like These* was still half-written, she was invited to be one of twelve women to address the provincial legislature. The Edmonton Equal Franchise League had organized a large delegation to present their case for female suffrage in the provincial legislature on February 15, 1915. Nellie felt completely at home among the stalwart, well-dressed Alberta matrons and their male supporters as they all marched up the stone steps to the legislature.

Part of Nellie McClung's skill as an advocate was that she tailored her arguments to her audience. She knew that the Liberal premier of Alberta, Arthur Lewis Sifton, was no huffing, puffing Sir Rodmond Roblin—Sifton was a cautious lawyer known for his integrity. She also knew that she was scheduled to speak last of the twelve suffrage speakers, perhaps because her new comrades recognized that she was the most eloquent, perhaps because others had more status in the province. So she carefully considered how to have most impact. As usual, this involved both an attractive new outfit (lace fichus were all the rage that year) and a canny sense of how to make her pitch. She skipped the maternal feminist arguments, and instead appealed to cabinet members' sense of natural justice. Her voice echoed through the building as she spoke: "I ask for no boon, no favour, no privilege. I am just asking for plain, old-fashioned, unfrilled justice." Alberta's leaders knew the great contribution that pioneer women had made in the West, working alongside and just as hard as their menfolk, and so they knew that it was only fair that women should have the vote. The *Edmonton Bulletin* described her address as "remarkable, not only for the many clever things that she said, but also for what she did not say."

The premier did not commit himself immediately to female suffrage. But in July the same year, Nellie saw one of her goals achieved: in a referendum on Prohibition, Albertans voted overwhelmingly to go "dry." Nellie herself had spoken all over the province in favour of Prohibition, and helped organize a mass rally in Edmonton. (The reluctance of some "respectable" women to march irked their courageous leader. "A parade brings to light a shocking condition of pedal infirmities—fallen arches—weak ankles—corns—ingrowing toe-nails—rheumatic joints," she wrote.) The *Edmonton Daily Bulletin* credited the "Ban the Bar" victory to the inspiration provided by the "untiring devotion, the greatest energy, the highest talent and the most abounding enthusiasm" of Mrs. McClung. The tide in favour of both Prohibition and women's suffrage now surged across the Prairies. By 1916, all three provinces had gone dry and granted women the right to vote in provincial elections.

One of the best photographs ever taken of Nellie McClung was snapped on April 19, 1916—the day the bill giving Alberta women the vote was read in the legislature. Sitting in the gallery were Nellie and two of her new Alberta friends, who were both magistrates (the first in the British Empire): Alice Jamieson from Calgary and Edmonton's Emily Murphy, well known on the prairies as the writer "Janey Canuck." Once the historic reading was done, the three women emerged triumphant into the chilly spring air, and linked arms as they strolled down Jasper Avenue. They were eager to celebrate, but Nellie's attachment to temperance ruled out champagne. Emily, a stout woman with what a contemporary described as "the lusty sea-going roll of a sailor," caught sight of a hat shop, and let out a whoop of glee. She shepherded her two friends through the door. Nellie chose a broad-brimmed hat decorated with a wide white ribbon and an enormous artificial flower, Alice selected a dignified bonnet with a velvet furbelow, and Emily plonked a feathered straw cloche on her head. Then the three women continued down the street to a photographer's studio. There they posed, resplendent in their thick wool coats and victory bonnets. The combination of middle-class respectability and quiet glee is endearing.

Other provinces took a little longer to give women the vote—British Columbia and Ontario in 1917; Nova Scotia in 1918; New Brunswick in 1919; Prince Edward Island in

1922; Newfoundland (an independent dominion) in 1925. In Quebec, where the Roman Catholic Church vehemently opposed the idea of female suffrage, the wait was much longer: women there did not win the vote until 1940.

At the same time, Conservative politicians in Ottawa realized the advantages of allowing some women to vote in federal elections. During the conscription crisis of 1917, Prime Minister Robert Borden granted the vote first to nurses at the front, then (in the Wartime Elections Act) to women born in Canada or Britain with close relatives in the armed forces. It was a Machiavellian tactic, spawned by the assumption that these women would vote in favour of conscription, and outweigh the votes of conscription critics in Quebec. Its devious purpose was obvious, since the act disenfranchised a couple of groups that had traditionally voted Liberal: conscientious objectors and people born in foreign countries and naturalized since 1902.

On this issue, Nellie found herself at odds with an old friend in Winnipeg. At first, she supported the idea that the vote should be given only to Canadian or British-born women closely related to soldiers. Jack was still alive, thank God, but he was still in the trenches and casualty lists grew longer every day. Of course more young men should be sent to Europe to fight alongside him and end hostilities. But

Francis Beynon promptly expressed her horror at Nellie's view in her *Grain Growers' Guide* column, reproaching Nellie for giving up on democracy when the going got tough. Nellie quickly admitted her mistake, as she wrote to her colleague, "because I place women's suffrage above all personal consideration and because I know that any one person's judgment is likely to be faulty." She grasped that the Borden government's tactics were divisive and regressive. "It is a matter for deep regret," she told a suffrage group in Calgary, "that any act should be passed which will make a cleavage in the ranks of our women citizens who are today bearing their full share of the burdens of life whether they happen to have relatives at the front or not. I hold firm to the belief that I would have been quite as good a citizen if my eldest child had been a girl, and quite as much interested in my country's welfare, but that fact would have put me outside the pale."

The following year, the Borden government went some way toward redeeming itself by giving most Canadian women the federal franchise. However, universal female suffrage did not arrive until after the Second World War, when women of Asian origin and registered Indian women (and men) were finally given the vote.

AS THE WAR PROGRESSED, women were well on their way to achieving Nellie McClung's two priorities: temperance and the vote. But Jack was still not home. "The war dragged out its dreary length," recalled Nellie in her memoirs, *The Stream Runs Fast*. On the map of France pinned to her kitchen wall, the family marked battle sites with black-headed pins. Cards or letters from Jack were read and reread. Nellie was frequently away from home, revving up campaigns for suffrage in both Canada and the United States, where women were still disenfranchised. She had made extensive speaking tours in Ontario and British Columbia in 1915, and was off to Minneapolis in early 1916. In the fall of that year, accompanied by seventeen-year-old Florence, she did a forty-city American tour, then continued on to Washington (via Wisconsin and Minnesota) for the National Convention of American suffragists in December 1916. There, according to a conference newsletter, "She kept her hearers wavering between laughter and tears as she hid her own emotions behind a veil of stoicism and humour." American women were finally allowed to cast their votes in federal elections in 1920.

Invitations from as far afield as New Zealand arrived at the McClung home. Although the suffrage movement had popular leaders in central Canada, including lawyer Clara Martin and physician Augusta Stowe Gullen, Nellie was now one of the best-known female activists in the world. A profile of this "Writer, Lecturer, Cake Baker, Politician, Methodist, Mother" appeared in *Canada Monthly* in February 1916. "Nellie McClung is the kind of personality you can't miss," observed the Toronto-based writer Natalie Symmes. "Drop her into a Canadian Club, a Press Club, a political meeting or her own Methodist Church and things begin to fizz. Most people like her. Some people don't. But everybody has to have an opinion of some sort, for she's as vivid as a tiger lily at a funeral." Symmes was blown away by Nellie's speaking skills. "If you've never heard Nellie McClung in action you can have no idea of how particularly Western, and how extraordinarily effective, her addresses are. . . . There she stands, arms akimbo, chin out. Round she sweeps and gives it to you with her right forefinger jabbing straight for your intellect. 'Woman's place is in the home, eh? Woman mustn't invade politics? But don't you know that woman isn't the invader? Politics has invaded the home.' . . . Nellie is some Chinook, eh, what?"

Nellie was equally busy on behalf of the boys at the front. She and her fellow activists threw themselves into raising money for the Red Cross and the Patriotic Fund: they held quilt sales and bake sales, sold subscriptions, toured northern Alberta giving speeches about the plight of prisoners of war in Germany. There was nothing Nellie liked better than getting out of the city, visiting towns that reminded her of Manitou, and meeting hard-working people (many of Ukrainian, Russian, or Chinese origin) with the simple rural values she cherished. She appears to have treated everybody with the same unpretentious warmth, regardless of race, creed, or their state of dress. When a shabbily dressed, elderly Cree man told a carload of Red Cross volunteers that his son was fighting in France, they quickly made room for him in the car. "We were all citizens of the British Empire; we were all of the great family of the Next-of-Kin, and after all, what is a dirty face and a torn coat?"

Some days it seemed that the war would never end. But Nellie, a natural optimist, began to think ahead, to the kind of Canada that women wanted once hostilities ceased. She silently cheered when women donned overalls to work on the land or in factories, replacing the men who had left to fight. She was exasperated by women who channelled their energies and anxieties into knitting—a make-work project that could be done by machines. As far as she was concerned, this was almost as bad as the "fatty degeneration of the conscience . . . that is disastrous to the development of thought," which she had railed against in *In Times Like These*. Women must *act*. With young men fighting overseas, there were labour shortages in schools, fields, and farm homes. Nellie was particularly concerned with the number of rural schools closing because of a teacher shortage. She told audiences that at least twenty thousand Alberta children would remain illiterate, many in "foreign settlements where already there is strong anti-British feeling." She wrote to Prime Minister Borden, suggesting he plug gaps in the labour market by mobilizing women on the home front as they had mobilized men to fight.

Nellie got the chance to make this argument in the spring of 1918. The Borden government convened a three-day Women's War Conference, and invited delegates from all over the country. A congenial but purposeful group of nineteen western delegates steamed across the country. In the rattling, plush-lined CPR carriages, old friends like Cora Hind from Winnipeg and newer acquaintances like Edmonton's Emily Murphy exchanged their own war stories and discussed strategies for dealing with Ottawa officials. Nellie stepped onto the platform at Ottawa's Union Station intent on raising two issues: the shortage of teachers, and the need to control the use of grain being exported to England, so that it wouldn't be converted to whiskey there.

On paper, the conference was an energy-charged explosion of fierce rhetoric and good resolutions. Nellie's ideas were fully aired, along with ideas for equal pay for equal work, a women's advisory lobby within government, a federal department of health, technical training for women, and a voluntary national register of women available for service. But in practice, most of the ideas went nowhere, and the western caucus was not impressed. About the only resolution that had any impact was the one urging daylight saving time as a conservation measure. Nellie groaned at the patronizing attitude of many of the male legislators. One man made the mistake of suggesting to her that the ladies must have enjoyed their holiday in the capital. Nellie drew herself up to her full five feet, four inches of height, and snorted. It had been a sense of duty, not desire for recreation, that had persuaded her to leave Wes and her children behind in Edmonton. "It is not a very easy thing for busy women to give up their work and take a long, tiresome journey to Ottawa."

On November 11, 1918, church bells across Canada pealed: war was over. Four months later, after nearly four years in Europe, Jack came home. The McClung residence had been spring-cleaned for the occasion, and eight-year-old Mark claimed his big brother's tin helmet and wore it for weeks. Physically, Jack, now twenty-two, was unharmed, but he had been traumatized by war. Nellie recorded that he had a "hurt look in his clear blue eyes" that "tore at my heart strings." He refused to speak of his experiences in the trenches: his brothers Paul and Horace, now eighteen and thirteen, found him so irritable and depressed that they called him "Iron Duke" behind his back. A well-meaning neighbour slapped him on the back and asked, "Well, young fellow, how does it feel to win a war?" Jack dropped his eyes and said in a quiet, bitter tone, "I did not know that wars were ever won. Certainly not by the people who do the fighting."

Nellie McClung grieved for her eldest son, but she had no time to waste. She had already developed feminist plans for the postwar world. "Women are at last admitted to every department of labor. . . . Women have gone into factories, offices, munition plants, everywhere that there was work to be done and even the bitterest critic has had to admit that they have made good! . . . And now the war is over, and people are anxiously asking, 'Will women go back?' . . . After you have driven your own car, will you be content to drive an ox in a Red River cart? . . . Women must claim the place they have won . . . in this new world that has been bought [at] such a price." Her first priority was that women should attend the peace conference in Paris.

Prime Minister Borden paid no attention. But Nellie had moved beyond her uncertainties of the early war years, and had a sense of what women activists wanted. And thanks to her and her friends, women now had the political power to push their concerns.

CHAPTER SEVEN

Did Nellie Ever Falter?

Edmonton and Calgary, 1919–1926

> I knew I could make a good speech. I knew
> I could persuade people . . . but I also
> knew that the whole situation was fraught
> with danger. . . . If a woman succeeded, her
> success would belong to her as an individual.
> People would say she was an exceptional
> woman . . . but if she failed, she failed for
> all women everywhere.

Each morning, in the McClungs' dining room, Wes would work his way through his bacon and eggs, their youngest son, Mark, would scramble onto his chair, and the family matriarch would entertain them with selections from the local newspaper. It was a bravissima performance. "She proclaimed the news, she declaimed the news, she exclaimed the news," recalled Mark in 1975. "It was always politics. She never paid any attention to the sports pages, or the social pages . . . [unless they] had to do with women. . . . But she would talk about whatever was happening in Edmonton politics, Alberta politics, Dominion politics, the League of Nations, whatever it was. . . . She really poured it out with great conviction. She would rattle the paper . . . with indignation or with pleasure, and those tiny hands of hers were very expressive. She would make them into fists and she would shake them when she was really moved. So, you know, you started the day with the feeling of participating in the world."

Nevertheless, the postwar world was a frustrating place for Nellie McClung. She wanted women to play a role in rebuilding the world, but she watched many women retreat from the labour force when their boys came home. She wanted women to keep pushing for minimum wages in sweatshops, equality under the law, more public nurses, and improved schools, but the momentum of the suffrage movement had evaporated. "Our forces, so well-organised for the campaign, began to dwindle," she noted. She might enjoy a jaunty hat or a swirly skirt, but she deplored the emergence of "flappers," with their short dresses and predilection for bridge, cocktails, and *thés dansants*. Moreover, she did not think that either the Liberal or the Conservative Party was the appropriate vehicle for feminists. When asked in 1917 if women should join a political party, she said, "Dividing the women into two hostile camps will leave the situation very much as we found it, with all of its old bitterness, squabbling and waste of energy. . . . I like to think of women forming their own opinions, uncontaminated by party hypotheses." She dreamt about a bloc of uncommitted women voters who would put their support behind any candidate who endorsed their priorities. In practice, this could prove embarrassing for candidates. In the 1915 Manitoba election campaign, she had appeared on a platform with one of the Conservative candidates and told the audience that he deserved to be elected because he had supported the Votes for Women campaign. But then she went on to trash the rest of his party and sing the praises of Liberals.

Despite her disregard for partisan loyalties, and her hell-raising reputation as the radical "Calamity Nell," Nellie McClung was no revolutionary. She might lead marches, but she believed in democracy. When labour leaders in Winnipeg called a general strike for May 15, 1919, she travelled to her old stomping ground to see the "strange things" going on there. For six torrid weeks, thirty thousand workers brought the city grinding to a halt. An unpublished account in her papers reveals that she was not impressed. She discovered that the strike leaders seemed "to have hypnotized themselves into the thought that nothing short of a social revolution and the overthrow of constitutional authority will save the world." Nellie had some sympathy for the labour movement, which had chalked up such victories as pay raises and shorter work days. She was willing to agree that the strikers' grievances were real. But she was appalled that the strikers dictated which newspapers, delivery wagons, and restaurants could operate, and who had access to gasoline. "There was something so despotic and arrogant about all this, that even indifferent citizens rallied to the call for help."

So Nellie found herself in a bind. She was eager for change, but she could not see how to achieve it. She could list off the initiatives a postwar government should take: "taxation of profits, the fixing of all prices, supervision of crops . . . better and cheaper housing, state care for the sick . . . old age pensions. . . ." But she also felt that "legislation is not enough—it is not new laws we need, it is a new spirit in our people—it is sometimes called a change of heart. No law or set of laws can bring peace to a world of grabbers." There was a whiff of hopeless blather in much of what she wrote and talked about for the next few months, as she implored women to kickstart a "change of spirit." Her speeches sounded increasingly like New Age sermons. "Woman's place in the new order is to bring imagination to work on life's problems. Without vision, which is another word for imagination, the people perish. It is vision that is needed now, rather than logic, and we have a right to expect it from women with their tender hearts and quick sympathies. We look to them to save the situation." An energetic pragmatist, she was adrift when grappling with abstract concepts. Her own son Mark once described his mother's approach to politics: "She'd tend to shy away from great abstract principles and she would always try to look at the individual need of the individual person."

Fortunately for Nellie, a figure was emerging on the federal political scene with whom she felt in sympathy. At first glance, the convergence of this western feminist with a Harvard-educated Toronto political scientist seems bizarre. But there was much about William Lyon Mackenzie King, elected leader of the Liberal Party in 1919, which appealed to her. One year younger than Nellie, he shared many of her late Victorian values: he was deeply sentimental and committed to social justice as a Christian ideal, and his credo was one that Nellie could have coined for herself: "Love Humanity." In addition, like Nellie, he knew that Canada must adapt to new economic forces. A well-respected labour negotiator, he had pushed for an eight-hour day and workers' compensation when he sat in Prime Minister Laurier's cabinet between 1908 and 1913 as minister of labour. Nellie was so impressed by King that she even waded her way through *Industry and Humanity*, his almost unreadable book about achieving industrial peace through co-operation instead of confrontation. She would watch him quietly assert control over Canada's internal and foreign policies in the 1920s—a decade of prosperity in Canada, when wheat sales soared, the railways boomed, and Ontario industry hummed.

But should Nellie take advantage of the opportunities she herself had helped create, and enter the political fray? Or should she remain on the outside of the electoral process, organizing street protests and grassroots conventions for the issues she cared about? Alberta could boast the first two women sitting in a Canadian legislative assembly: Louise McKinney and Roberta MacAdams had both been elected in 1917. Now Nellie played with the idea of joining them. She declined to run federally because Mark was still only ten and, as she told her friend Agnes Laut, "still needed a mother's constant care and love." But when an election was called in Alberta for July 18, 1921, the forty-seven-year-old activist agreed to run in Edmonton for the governing Liberals, who were confident of re-election. She told the *Edmonton Journal* that she was running only after "very careful and reluctant consideration, because she could foresee a chance of serving women more than in the past." Nevertheless, her spirits soared as, once again, she stood facing enthusiastic crowds, talking about her two favourite issues—women's rights and the need to enforce Prohibition. A seat in cabinet, from which she could have real influence, appeared within her grasp.

The 1921 provincial election was a personal triumph for Nellie: she joined the tiny band of women who had won seats in provincial or federal legislatures. The same year, Agnes Macphail became the first woman elected to the House of Commons in Ottawa. But in Alberta, Nellie was the only woman within a shrunken Liberal caucus. To the complete shock of observers, an upstart new party called the United Farmers of Alberta (UFA) formed the government. Nellie's victory speech was muted: "Too many good men and women have gone down to defeat today for me to be bubbling over with joy at this time."

A highlight for Nellie during these years was the alliance she forged on some issues with the only other woman in the legislature—UFA member Irene Parlby, who had been appointed to the cabinet. One such occasion arose when a Conservative MLA argued that married women whose husbands earned a good wage should not be in the paid workforce. "Mrs. Parlby and I were able to head off this piece of sex prejudice," Nellie recalled, vindicated in her conviction that women should cross party lines on issues that affected women. The two women also co-operated on two resolutions that were sent to Ottawa, one in support of equal treatment for men and women in divorce proceedings, and the other recommending that a woman's citizenship should not be affected by her marriage.

One issue that Nellie championed was the right of parents to sterilize mentally handicapped children. In her memoirs, Nellie characteristically uses an anecdote to explain the rationale for Alberta's Sexual Sterilization Act, which eventually became law in 1928. She describes a "poor distracted mother from southern Alberta" who had an eighteen-year-old daughter with the intellect of a six-year-old. Various unsavoury men had started hanging around the girl, and the mother was crazy with worry that her daughter would get pregnant. But the surgery was performed, and a year later the child had happily taken charge of the chickens and, to Nellie's satisfaction, was doing "Norwegian knitting . . . the home was happy again."

This attitude to mental disability shocks contemporary readers because we see it as prejudice against the disabled, and an invasion of human rights. In the 1920s, however, it was regarded as an enlightened concern about the physical and intellectual strength of the population. Eugenics, or the "science" of selective breeding, had been growing in popularity ever since Charles Darwin's cousin Francis Dalton had first coined the term in 1883. A University of Toronto psychologist, W.G. Smith, triggered a wave of horror in 1920 when he reported, without any documented evidence, that the United States rejected 1 in every 1,590 immigrants as a "mental defective," whereas Canada's rejection rate was 1 in every 10,127 immigrants. Was sterling Canadian stock being swamped by the "wrong sort of foreigners," especially after so many of the "right sort" (a euphemism for Anglo-Saxons) had been massacred in the First World War?

Several of Nellie's friends were much more outspoken than she was on the subject. Emily Murphy, the magistrate whom Nellie had met in Edmonton, was a fervent supporter of forced sterilization, saying, "We protect the public against diseased and distempered cattle. We should similarly protect them against the offal of humanity." She insisted that "insane people are not entitled to progeny," and made the totally unsubstantiated claim that 4 percent of the population of Alberta were either "feeble-minded" or insane. "A large proportion of these patients," she announced, "could not be taught to chew gum without swallowing it."

Ontario's pioneer of public health, Dr. Helen MacMurchy, was also pro-eugenics, because she firmly believed that the "feeble-minded" threatened the nation's health. Such concerns were shared by progressive British thinkers, such as George Bernard Shaw and Sidney and Beatrice Webb. It was only after the public learned of the horrific lengths to which Nazi Germany had taken the idea of improving human stock that serious doubts were raised about Alberta's Sexual Sterilization Act. But the act was not repealed until 1972, by which date 2,822 Albertans had been sterilized for reasons varying from low IQ to promiscuity. Nellie's support for eugenics, reflecting the conventional wisdom of her era, demonstrates how conventional wisdom may not be wise.

Nellie's five years as an opposition MLA were not happy ones, because she did not have the personality for parliamentary rules and process. As she admitted in her memoirs, "I was not a good party woman, and I'm sure there were times when I was looked upon with disfavour." Her Liberal colleagues found her maddening because if she thought that government initiatives had merit, she voted for them. She supported a UFA bill permitting unmarried mothers to sue the father of the child for maintenance, and revisions to the Dower Act to benefit women who had "trouble with their husbands." But she voted against a minimum wage act because it didn't permit women to sit on the administrative board, and she resisted government attempts to reduce allowances to widows and deserted wives who were single parents. I can imagine the men around her rolling their eyes as she had the nerve to argue that if anything was to be cut, it should not be allowances to the needy but the stipend of two thousand dollars a year that she and her fellow MLAs received.

Most disappointing for Nellie was the way anti-Prohibitionists were destroying all the hard work she had put into the "Ban the Bar" campaigns. Her opponents (they styled themselves "The Moderation League") developed a nifty new strategy and rallying cry. They argued that Prohibition was forcing Albertans to drink in secret within their own homes, putting wives and children at risk and making bootleggers rich. Nellie rehearsed her refutation of these arguments in an unpublished paper, "How Prohibition Is Working in Canada." She claimed that the problem was not a bad law, but inadequate enforcement. "Crime has decreased eighty percent, arrests for drunkenness have practically disappeared, jails have become empty, and inebriate farms have been sold because there were no inebriates to be cared for." Maybe men were finding the law difficult, but "the women and children are not saying a word against it!"

Was she right? Prairie historian James Gray confirms that Prohibition had indeed transformed life in the West. Liquor consumption *was* reduced by 80 percent, convictions for drunkenness fell precipitously across the Prairies, and during the first month of Prohibition in Alberta, according to the *Edmonton Bulletin*, Alberta savings accounts rose by 100 percent. "With the pauperizing effect of unrestrained boozing removed," according to Gray, "a new tranquility came to family life in the cities and towns."

But the tide of public opinion had turned against Prohibition, and despite Nellie's campaigns, in a 1923 referendum, Prohibition was voted down in Alberta. Public sales and consumption of alcohol once again became legal. "We have slipped, we have failed, we have gone back and no one who has made an intelligent study of the question . . . can have any feeling but sorrow," a downhearted Nellie told the legislature. Her famous sense of humour was entirely invisible on this issue, about which she felt so strongly. In fact, her language was so full of fire and brimstone that she sounds like the worst kind of holy roller. "The Nation which deliberately chooses the path of self-indulgence and appetite does not always get a second chance. Babylon, Rome, Greece laughed at the 'sore heads' who warned them that they were pursuing the path which would lead to destruction."

The alcohol issue was of particular poignancy for Nellie McClung. She had been unable to campaign against the 1923 referendum because she had been in Banff, where Wes was in a sanatorium. The nature of his illness was never specified: was it a recurrence of the problem that had forced him to sell the Manitou pharmacy in 1906? At the same time, Nellie knew that drink was becoming a problem within her own family. On one occasion Paul had smashed the family car after a night out; by the time her sons were adults, according to Mark McClung, all four had drinking problems. This was a particularly cruel situation for Canada's best-known temperance crusader, who worried constantly that gossip about her sons would undermine her efforts.

It cannot have been easy being Nellie's husband or child: she was a high-energy individual who, by the time she was middle-aged, was very sure of her opinions. She was used to being the centre of attention: her intensity, even when masked in humour, did not allow much room for other personalities to blossom around her. And she was so beloved by her fans that her children, however proud they were of her, must have felt splinters of resentment toward the smothering public figure who, they kept being told, was so special. What young man would feel unalloyed contentment to have such a controversial woman as his mother, or feel completely comfortable being "Our Nellie's son" rather than his own person? Moreover, Nellie's sons may have resented their father's apparent meekness in the face of their mother's dynamism. Eula Lapp, a school friend of Nellie's son Horace, once recalled a Christmas Eve visit to the McClung household in Calgary in the 1920s, during which everybody had "a jolly time" in front of an open fire. Throughout the evening, however, "Wes was busy, just as if no one else were there—mending shirts! I don't mean that he was rude, nor uncommunicative; but he went ahead with a job that he wanted done." Mrs. Lapp admired the way that "there was no suggestion from him, nor from Nellie, that there was anything out-of-the-ordinary for a man to spend Christmas Eve at home with his friends, mending shirts." But it was out of the ordinary, and teenage sons never appreciate their parents being "different." The McClung boys probably found such role reversal embarrassing.

Was alcohol a form of rebellion? There was a dark side to McClung family dynamics. And Nellie could certainly be overbearing, but her private life remains private. Although she drew on a considerable archive for her own cheerful memoirs, her daughter, Florence (who did not inherit her mother's zeal or charisma), burnt most of the letters and all the lengthy diaries that her mother had accumulated. Family secrets went up in flames, and we can only speculate about Wes's sporadic health problems, or about the pervasive alcoholism in the family. Nellie's family chose to present to the world the same relentlessly upbeat personality that Nellie herself exuded in public, and reflected in her fiction. It is, however, significant that her children usually preferred to live at some distance from her.

Despite family tensions, Nellie herself continued her crusade. Alberta's Liquor Control Act of 1924 permitted the

reopening of bars for the sale of beer, and established govern-
ment-controlled liquor stores. She agitated for temperance
literature to be displayed alongside the sale of alcohol, and
also for the proceeds of liquor sales to go toward welfare and
old-age pensions. The government's decision to run the
stores at a profit, and to allow liquor advertising, gave her
"the jolt of her life." Her suspicion that politics was immoral
was confirmed: the government had launched itself into the
liquor business, she decided, purely to make money.

Alberta went to the polls again in 1926, and this time Nellie
ran in a Calgary riding. Three years earlier, the McClungs had
moved to Calgary because Wes had been transferred to the
Manufacturers' Life Insurance office there. But Nellie was not
so well known in this city, and her Prohibition rants turned off
voters. When she heard she had not won the seat, she pretend-
ed she didn't care. "I went about quite lightheartedly and gay,
telling myself and others how fine it felt to be free, and . . . how
glad I was that I could go back to my own work with a clear
conscience." She plunged into an orgy of cooking. "I grated
cheese, stoned dates, blanched almonds, whipped cream, set
jelly—and let the phone ring! It could tear itself out by the
roots for all I cared. I was in another world, the pleasant, land-
locked, stormless haven of double-boilers, jelly moulds, flour
sifters and other honest friends who make no promise they

cannot carry through. . . . No woman can turn out an ovenful of flaky pies, crisply browned, and spicily odorous, and not find peace for her troubled soul!" Her husband and children probably took refuge as they heard the matriarch beat the living daylight out of the egg whites.

The next day, the manager of Calgary's tony Earl Grey Golf Club was surprised to see a stocky woman teeing off with surprising vigour. At regular intervals she would look up at the distant, snow-capped mountains; more frequently, she kept her head down and appeared to be talking to each ball before she took a vicious swing at it. The same woman appeared for the following two days, too, and often cast an angry look at the mansions in the posh Elbow Park neighbourhood at the course's edge. "I played each morning," wrote Nellie later, "and did some splendid driving by naming the balls, and was able by that means to give one or two of them a pretty powerful poke."

Nellie blamed liquor interests for her defeat, along with those men who believed that "public offices, particularly those that carry emoluments," should belong exclusively to men. The defeat stung—but there were compensations. Now she would not have to leave her family for weeks at a time, when the legislature was sitting. The McClung home, at 803 15th Avenue SW, was rapidly emptying, and Nellie wanted to revel in every moment she still had children at home. Jack had completed a degree at the University of Alberta and had moved on to Oxford University. Florence was now married and living in Regina. Paul had disappeared south as soon as he could leave school, and would settle in Texas; in 1925, Wes and Nellie visited him there. In 1926, only twenty-year-old Horace and fifteen-year-old Mark were still in Calgary. Nellie spent many hours at her desk in her second-floor bedroom, writing or dictating to her assistant, Winnie Fudger. But then she would hear the front door open, and she would be out of her chair in a flash. "I can see her now," Fudger recalled in 1977 for authors Mary Hallett and Marilyn Davis. "It didn't matter when those boys came in—from school or from work or wherever . . . she'd run half way down those stairs, and they'd run up, 'Hello, mother dear,' and they'd embrace each other. I don't think they ever failed to do that."

Since Winnipeg days, Nellie had relied on a series of live-in maids for household help. Most were newly arrived immigrants, often from Central Europe, who washed, ironed, cleaned, and cooked for a salary of about twenty dollars a week. Many young women in similar circumstances were ruthlessly exploited, and left domestic service for employment in factories as soon as they could. Nellie looked after "my girls." She made their friends welcome, helped them learn

English, took them with her to church every Sunday, introduced them to guests, and allowed them to entertain their suitors in the front room. "Little privileges like these help a girl to know that she is a person of importance with the protection and dignity of a family and a home." She also listened to their stories, knowing they were the perfect raw material for her fiction. The heroine of one of her most popular novels, *Painted Fires*, is a Finnish domestic called Helmi Milander.

There may have been fewer children around, but there were just as many visitors. Nellie's hospitality around her old-fashioned dining-room table was legendary. Shy young women from church, old friends from Manitoba, visiting politicians and authors were all welcome. Agnes Macphail, Canada's first woman MP, was struck by the way Nellie put everybody at ease. "Often when someone has been greatly praised all our expectations are not fulfilled. But Nellie McClung was just what I expected her to be," she told a reporter after a visit. "I liked her immensely and oddly enough felt that I had known her always." Macphail warmed to Wes, too. "We do not hear so much about him, but he is worth hearing a good deal about. . . . He is a man of substance, mentally and physically . . . he is proud of his wife's achievements."

Nellie McClung never again ran for elected office after her 1926 defeat. In 1930, Mackenzie King wanted her to run in a high-profile battle against Conservative leader R.B. Bennett in Calgary: "It would be a fine thing to have you in Parliament," he coaxed. But she knew her limitations: her years as a parliamentarian had revealed her inability to be a team player or to allow others to take the limelight. Although she remained a Liberal, she knew she was more effective pressing the system from the outside for the changes she wanted, rather than trying to fit inside it. However, she and four allies would soon have a big impact on the Canadian Parliament.

CHAPTER EIGHT

If Women Aren't Persons, What the Heck Are We?

Calgary, 1926–1932

> Public offices, particularly those that carry
> emoluments, they believe to belong, by the
> ancient right of possession, to men. They are
> quite willing to let women work on boards, or
> committees, or indeed anywhere if the work is
> done gratuitously—but if there is a salary, they
> know at once that women are not fitted by nature
> for that! . . . And the curious part of this is that
> women can be found who will support this view.
> Not many—and not thinking women—just a few
> who bitterly resent having any woman go farther
> than they are ever likely to go.

Nellie McClung was never one to brood. "There is no use
sitting by the dead ashes of yesterday's fire," she often told
friends. "Take the minutes as read and get on with the next
order of business." She was now fifty-three, and though she
was a little stouter and slower these days, her smile was as
bright and her energy level as high as ever. That was just as

well, since she belonged to practically every women's organization in the province—the Women's Institute, the Women's Press Club, the Women's Missionary Society, the Local Council of Women, the Canadian Authors Association, and the Women's Canadian Club. (Alberta women were tireless in their determination to improve the world. Nellie quoted in her memoirs the *Calgary Herald* columnist who noted that even in heaven you would be able to pick out Alberta women because they would be the ones "in little groups with pencils and notebooks, by the side of the river of life, giving the finishing touches to resolution B. 72894 urging that more rural children be taken into the Heavenly Choirs.")

These organizations were proud to have Nellie's name on their letterhead because she worked so hard, and because she was a Canadian star, celebrated for both political and literary achievement. Between 1921 and 1931, "Our Nell," as her fans called her, published six books, plus countless short stories. Nellie's fiction continued to sell well, although her style was dated. Committed to the late Victorian idea that storytelling had a high moral purpose, Nellie continued to write about family abuse, alcoholism, racial prejudice, illegitimacy, and the death of overworked wives owing to lack of medical attention. Their author was impatient with the modernist fiction of younger writers like Katherine Mansfield and Virginia Woolf, which featured interior monologues reflecting the growing influence of psychoanalysis. In the fall of 1920, the eager young Toronto editor Lorne Pierce of Ryerson Press had sent her a book called *Woman* by Madeleine Marx. In reply, Nellie didn't mince her words: "These intensely subjective stories, where the heroine is always spreading her feelings on the table and analyzing them and minutely describing them, have always struck me as being decidedly unwholesome and purposeless. In fact the outstanding feature of the whole book to me is the lack of purpose in this woman's life. I cannot see that she brought any understanding or comfort or guidance into the lives of any of the people she met, and certainly her experiment is not what one would care to recommend to the Girl Guides or the Canadian Girls in Training."

Nellie's journalism was another matter. Here, she was ahead of the crowd, chivvying women to take public roles. Her essay "What Have We Gained in Sixty Years?" was published in the *Canadian Home Journal* in 1927: her answer was "not enough." "Can a Woman Raise a Family and Have a Career?" she asked in *Maclean's* magazine in 1928, and—no surprise—answered her own question in a rousing affirmative. A husband's moral support helps, she wrote, and home and children must never be neglected. Nevertheless, "I believe that a woman who has done something outside her home acquires a wider viewpoint, which in turn is passed on to her children."

But there were so many barriers to women in public life. Since before the 1914–18 war, Nellie McClung had campaigned for the ordination of women within the Methodist Church. A woman of rock solid faith herself, who marched her whole household (including domestics) off to church every Sunday, she objected strongly to the fact that women did so much of the work of the church, yet were denied equality both in its councils and in the pulpit. "Woman has the same relation to the church," she sniped, "as the hole to the donut." Female ordination was more than a matter of employment equity, in her view: it was a matter of fundamental Christian doctrine. "Christ was a true democrat," she wrote in 1916. "He was a believer in women, and never in his life did he discriminate against them." One of her most pointed verses on this subject appeared in *In Times Like These*. Entitled "A Heart to Heart Talk with the Women of the Church by the Governing Bodies," it read,

> Go, labor on, good sister Anne,
> Abundant may thy labors be;
> To magnify thy brother man
> Is all the Lord requires of thee!

Go raise the mortgage, year by year,
And joyously thy way pursue,
And when you get the title clear,
We'll move a vote of thanks to you!

Go, labor on, the night draws nigh;
Go, build us churches—as you can.
The times are hard, but chicken-pie
Will do the trick. Oh, rustle, Anne!

Go, labor on, good sister Sue,
To home and church your life devote;
But never, never ask to vote,
Or we'll be very cross with you!

Demanding the ordination of women in early twentieth-century Canada was as much as a challenge to the establishment as demanding the vote. Back then, church ministers, whether Anglican, Methodist, Presbyterian, Congregationalist, or Roman Catholic, were community leaders; most Canadians attended church, particularly in rural areas; and the word of God cut a mighty swathe. We can glimpse the resistance that Nellie faced, in her struggle with the Methodist hierarchy, if we look at the resistance within the Roman Catholic Church today to married priests (let alone women priests).

It was an uphill struggle. The arguments against women's ordination ranged from doctrinal to trivial. In one Calgary debate, her opponent, a Dr. W.A. Lewis, recounted how he had once had to pull his horse and buggy out of a muddy slough without dirtying his suit before church. A woman minister would never be able to cope with such challenges, he intoned. Nellie promptly retorted that a woman would have been practical enough to wear old clothes and keep her good clothes in a bag if the mud was that bad.

But Dr. Lewis was part of a much bigger picture—the inertia of the ecclesiastical establishment. While Nellie was still living in Edmonton, back in 1921, she had glimpsed this when she was selected to be one of the twenty-four Canadian delegates (and the only woman) to the Fifth Ecumenical Methodist Conference in England. She was honoured to be invited, although her housekeeper, Mrs. Fuller, worried that Nellie's table manners were not up to scratch. The two women sat at the McClung kitchen table, with Nellie chortling as she learned to hold her fork like a pen rather than a dagger, and to eat a boiled egg with irreproachable *délicatesse*.

This was Nellie's first trip to the "mother country," and everything was a surprise—although some surprises were less pleasant than others. At the opening banquet in the Cecil

Hotel, a magnificent eight hundred–room palace on the Strand, she was horrified to see delegates from the southern United States refuse to sit beside delegates from the African Methodist Church. All Nellie's innate egalitarianism rose to the surface. She quickly bustled over, sat down on one of the vacated chairs, and started chatting with the African delegates about the state of Methodism in their land. Next, she listened to a dreary, pretentious speech from a British grandee called Sir Robert Pearkes. She didn't record what he spoke about, only that he used "some crackling big words." (She also noted that "the brightest spot of the evening was Lady Pearkes' diamonds.") The dinner seemed to go on forever, and gave Nellie an unpleasant taste of both British food and British snobbery.

By the eighth day of the conference, Nellie McClung was shuddering at the self-satisfied apathy. Her only opportunity to talk came when she was asked to respond to a worthy address on the subject of "The Awakening of Women." The other participants probably regarded her, up to this point, as a lively but homely woman from the unknown vastness of Canada, but they soon learned she was more than that. First of all, Nellie tore apart the title of the session. Women had never been asleep, she said: their lack of interest in politics was because they were too busy. Women, she went on, had spent the last fifty years feeding, clothing, and raising their families without the help of any labour-saving devices. She soon moved on to her hobby horse: the ordination of women. There was no sweet deference to the male point of view as she reproached her fellow delegates for simultaneously refusing to accept women into the pulpit while failing to engage the interest of the postwar generation of women. "Does it never occur to [church ministers] that though they have failed to reach the women, some one else might be more successful?" The church ministers stared at her, stony-faced, and many of the other delegates whispered about this woman's cheek. But those members of the press who had been as bored as Nellie by many of the speeches loved her: one reporter called her "racy, delightfully frank, and above all reasonable."

Nellie was captivated by London itself. Like any self-respecting tourist, she ticked off the main sights—the Changing of the Guard at Buckingham Palace, Big Ben, the House of Lords. She complained to her landlady about the cold, and the latter fluttered, "I never will understand the colonials." Nellie also visited France, to see for herself the killing fields of the war. The experience for her was exactly the same as for every subsequent visitor—twenty, fifty, eighty years later. As she walked up and down the acres and acres of white crosses, a wave of desolation and horror swept over her. On Vimy Ridge, she stooped and lifted out a handful of earth. It was a gruesome moment for a woman who, only three years earlier, had been following the news from the front with dread. "A button met my touch; a button attached to a piece of grey cloth. I put it back hastily for I was not hunting for souvenirs."

When Nellie got home, she found that her Methodist friends were now consumed with another issue: the union of the Methodist, Congregationalist, and Presbyterian churches. After the United Church was established in 1925, Nellie relaunched her campaign for female ordination—and now she had a candidate. A young woman from Saskatchewan named Lydia Gruchy presented herself for ordination in 1928. She had all the right educational and personal qualifications: in addition to a degree in theology, according to Nellie, she could "play the organ, lead the singing, drive a car, keep house, hold her tongue and get along with people." How many male ministers, one wonders, shared all these traits? Nellie sat in the United Church annual assembly that year, grinning with anticipation that at last the fortress would be breached. She drummed her fingers impatiently as various church bodies brought in their reports. Across the aisle an elderly minister who supported the idea of women ministers gave her an encouraging smile. But a nasty surprise was coming. The head of the Women's Missionary Society interrupted her catalogue of good works at home and abroad, lifted her head, and spoke directly to the church's moderator: "You have not asked us what we think of the ordination of women—and it is just as well. You will find us very conservative."

Nellie gaped in horror. "That was all—but it was enough!" Across the aisle, her ally looked at her sadly, and drew his forefinger across his throat. "He knew the day was lost, and I knew it too. . . ." Nellie thought of all the empty churches that needed ministers, and all the women with the ability to lead congregations. Female ordination, she reflected privately, "will come, of course. In the meantime, it makes me sad at heart to think that the church has been the last stronghold of prejudice. Every other profession has opened its doors, and women have entered, some to succeed, some to fail, thus proving their humanity. . . . I know the church in its conservatism [is] losing great leaders who would [grace] the ministry and do much to make the church a greater force than it has been. . . ." One such "great leader," it goes without saying, would have been Nellie herself. Her son Mark always said his mother would have made a "humdinger of a clergyman. She would have filled the churches." Instead, she had to wait until 1936 before the United Church finally accepted the ordination of women, and Lydia Gruchy was appointed to be minister at St. Andrew's United Church in Moose Jaw.

THE CHURCH was not the only stronghold of prejudice, and after Nellie lost her seat in the Alberta legislature, one of her allies from the Prohibition battles gave her another target. Edmonton magistrate Emily Murphy had been campaigning for years to get another institution to open its doors to women: the federal Senate. However, her petitions went nowhere in Ottawa because first Prime Minister Robert Borden, and then Prime Minister Arthur Meighen, argued that the 1867 British North America Act ruled out such an appointment. Section 24 of the act stated that only "quali-fied persons" might be called to the Senate, and a British court had ruled that women were "persons in matters of pains and penalties, but not persons in matters of rights and privileges."

Emily Murphy had a great advantage in her campaign. She had three brothers who were all lawyers, and eager to help their bulldozer of a sister. So, on their advice, Murphy tried a different tack. A clause in the Supreme Court Act stated that any five interested citizens could petition for an interpretation of any part of the BNA Act, if the minister of justice supported the request for a ruling. In 1927, Murphy invited Nellie McClung, Irene Parlby (still a minister in the Alberta government), Louise McKinney (head of the WCTU), and Henrietta Muir Edwards (a co-founder of the National Council of Women) to join her in petitioning the Supreme Court.

In August that year, there was a formidable gathering of Canada's foremost social reformers on the verandah of Emily's Edmonton home. None of the five feminists was a shrinking violet, but Emily Murphy was the exuberant leader. As a friend noted in the Toronto *Mail and Empire* after her death, "She was abundantly blessed with the love of humour. Her laughter, which was frequent, was no lady-like titter, but something spontaneous and free and full-throated." Bees droned in the delphiniums and roses as the women planned their strategy. In various speeches, Nellie had already made her views on the Senate clear. "It is high time to get new blood into the moribund body, the Canadian Senate," she told one crowd. "The old men lack imagination." But the Murphy strategy called for cool logic rather than colourful rhetoric. After much humorous repartee and serious haggling over wording, a question was developed and a pre-eminent litigator approached.

Newton Rowell, an Ontario lawyer who strongly supported the goals of the women who hired him (his own wife had helped form women's associations within the Liberal Party), agreed to take the case. The province of Alberta lent its support to the women's case. Moreover, Mackenzie King's minister of justice, Ernest Lapointe, not only agreed that the eligibility question should be referred to the Supreme Court, but also undertook to pay the five women's legal costs. Although conservative on many issues (divorce, for example, was anathema to him), Lapointe was progressive on issues of women's political rights. He was appalled that women in his home province of Quebec were still denied the vote, and he sympathized with the struggles of Quebec suffragists such as Thérèse Casgrain.

It was a surprise for Toronto feminists that this initiative had come out of the West. "I hear," Emily wrote to Nellie, "that it has been a terrible shock to the Eastern women that five coal heavers and plough pushers from Alberta went over their heads to the Supreme Court without even saying, 'Please ma'am can we do it?'" But as Nellie had demonstrated in Manitoba, women in western Canada had a far greater sense of entitlement than women in the cities of central Canada. They had broken the prairie sod alongside their husbands, and worked just as hard to settle the Dominion's vast landscape. Why shouldn't they have a say in the country's future?

In March 1928, Rowell presented the question to Canada's Supreme Court. "Does the word 'Person' in section 24 of the British North America Act, 1867, include female persons?" To a modern ear, accustomed to nonsexist language, the answer is so obvious that it is hard to see the need for judicial discussion. If women aren't persons, what are we? But to a society only just emerging from the woman-as-subspecies era, the answer was not self-evident. And on April 24, 1928, Chief Justice Anglin handed down an opinion that reflected that thinking. The British North America Act must be interpreted precisely the way it was intended when it was passed. Since no women held public office in 1867, the act's authors could not have had any intention of including women among those eligible for the Senate. The Jesuit-educated Anglin established the perfect tautology: women were barred from sitting in the Senate because they had never done so. They had never done so because they were barred. Prime Minister King confided to his diary that Anglin was "a laughing stock and an ass."

Murphy and company were stunned but undaunted. There was a further court of last resort in those days. The Judicial Committee of the Privy Council in Westminster could hear an appeal, and Newton Rowell was dispatched to London to plead the case there. The federal government showed its support for the Alberta women by, once again, agreeing to cover the costs. (Nellie personally credited Mackenzie King for this support, although it was, once again, his Quebec lieutenant Ernest Lapointe who committed Ottawa. Initially, Lapointe had considered a constitutional amendment to secure women the right to sit in the Senate, but he switched tactics when he realized that Quebec, still deeply conservative and Catholic, would never accept such an amendment.) In October 1929, after four days of hearings, the British lord chancellor, Lord Sankey, rose to the full measure of his bewigged height and announced that "the exclusion of women from all public offices is a relic of days more barbarous than ours." The BNA Act, he said, was "planted in Canada, a living tree capable of growth and expansion within its natural limits." The judicial committee preferred a liberal interpretation of the act, rather than the narrow, technical view espoused by the Canadian judiciary. In some clauses, the BNA Act clearly meant the word "persons" to include women, so why shouldn't it in the section dealing with the Senate? "Their lordships have come to the conclusion," intoned the lord chancellor, "that the word 'persons' includes members of the male and female sex, and that therefore . . . women are eligible to be summoned and become members of the Senate of Canada."

The Privy Council's decision, in the words of legal scholars Robert J. Sharpe and Patricia I. McMahon, "was a bold legal step." It reflected the progressive spirit of the Jazz Age rather than the legal status quo preferred by the Canadian legal establishment. Its broader legacy was to recognize the BNA Act as an enduring and flexible "living tree" intended to reflect changes over time.

On October 18, 1929, as Nellie recorded in her memoirs, "newspapers all over the British Empire carried black headlines: 'Privy Council Declares That Women Are Persons!' The London *Daily Telegraph* called the decision "a significant advance towards the equality of political rights for both sexes which is sometimes, quite erroneously, supposed to be already the rule of the civilized worlds." The London *Evening Standard* suggested that the judgment "will have an indirect bearing on the political activities of women throughout the Empire." Meanwhile, in Canada, the *Toronto Daily Star*'s headline read, "Canadian Women Win Right to Senate Seats." (Editors at the Toronto *Globe*, on the other hand, showed a typical skepticism about anything not generated in Toronto: they relegated the story to page six.)

The news was not all good. Many prominent women, including Agnes Macphail, the first woman MP, applauded the moral victory but moved quickly on to a more fundamental issue: what was the point of the Canadian Senate anyway? And although Prime Minister King made all the right noises about the decision as a great victory, he dragged his feet about naming a woman to the Senate. It was an open secret that Emily Murphy wanted to be the first woman in the Red Chamber, but she was far too mouthy for cautious Mr. King. Besides, she was a Conservative. And for all King's encouragement of Nellie McClung's electoral ambition, he didn't really want "Our Nell" in the Senate, refusing to accept party discipline and stirring things up. Instead, he turned to a woman of irreproachable Liberal credentials and traditional femininity. Cairine Wilson was the daughter of a wealthy Liberal senator, wife of a Liberal MP, and mother of eight children. One newspaper editorial took a swipe at Nellie McClung and her colleagues as it noted approvingly,

> A lady of retiring disposition, of refinement and culture, Senator Wilson's interest in public affairs has never been tinged with the desire for personal recognition or advancement: it had little appeal for a lady of station, and she took no part in the agitation for the recognition of women's right to

sit in the Senate. . . . It is eminently fitting that she should be the first appointee rather than one of the very industrious women politicians, spinsters, and others, who have talked incessantly of their rights as women without discharging any of their responsibilities as such.

Women senators, apparently, had to adhere to completely different standards than their male seatmates. In the opinion of the editorialist, one of Wilson's greatest virtues was that she had "never permitted her political interests to interfere with those other, and perhaps greater, responsibilities of citizenship, her duties as wife and mother."

Nonetheless, the group now known as the "Famous Five" had scored a famous victory in the struggle for equality before the law. Was it more than symbolic? The Privy Council's decision did not change attitudes overnight. As Nellie had noted in the *Canadian Home Journal*, "Sex prejudice and the male superiority complex, built up since time began, will not go out in one generation." In print and in speeches, she continued to rail against barriers that still remained—the difficulties facing women who wanted postsecondary educations, the ban against women who operated their own businesses joining the Calgary Board of Trade, the resistance to women in the workforce. She also expressed her exasperation with the way that women themselves were slow to take advantage of new opportunities. "We must try to convince women . . . that if they claim equality, they must play fair; that they cannot make economic dependence, which no longer exists, an excuse for letting men pay their bills; that they must look for no favours or special privileges, but with dignity, courtesy and straightforwardness go in and possess the land, or at least their share of it."

Nellie wanted gender equality, in politics, the church, business, public opinion. Yes, women were persons, but those who claimed their rights were too often dismissed as unfeminine freaks. "We may yet live to see the day when women will no longer be news," she wrote wistfully in December 1929. "And it cannot come too soon. I want to be a peaceful, happy, normal human being, pursuing my unimpeded way through life, never having to stop to explain, defend or apologize for my sex. . . . I am tired of belonging to the sex that is called the Sex."

Nine years later, Nellie was the sole member of the Famous Five present at the only formal commemoration of their victory. In June 1938, she took the train across Canada to Ottawa's Union Station, across from the green copper roofs of the Château Laurier. The next day was sticky and hot as the sixty-five-year-old crusader walked up to Parliament

Hill and into the fan-vaulted coolness of the Centre Block's Hall of Remembrance. Nellie wore an elegant dark evening dress with a shiny silver buckle on her belt. Her black leather shoes pinched, but her silver curls were arranged neatly around that broad forehead. She was quite the match for Prime Minister Mackenzie King, who appeared for the occasion in white tie and tails and looked distinctly nervous in the official photograph, surrounded by formidably regal women.

The Business and Professional Women of Canada had placed a plaque in the lobby of the Senate, commemorating the Persons Case. Three of the five women (Henrietta Muir Edwards, Louise McKinney, and Emily Murphy) had already died. Irene Parlby had declined the invitation; instead, she listened to the ceremony on her radio at her farm in Alex, Alberta. In front of three hundred senators, MPs, and representatives of women's groups, Nellie stood proudly at the prime minister's left as he unveiled the plaque. King's speech was predictable, stuffy, and laboured. Then Nellie herself stepped forward, and from the first word she uttered had her listeners entranced. She talked about the long campaign to "convince the world [women] had souls, and then that they had minds," and then that they deserved the right to political office. She paid a loyal tribute to her fellow members of the Famous Five, but with characteristic impatience added,

"We would all be able to accomplish a great deal more if none of us cared who got the credit." And she alerted the prime minister that she was ready for the next battle: "The end is not yet!"

Fighting words—but, as it turned out, a touch empty. Days after Lord Sankey spoke, the New York stock market crashed, ushering in the Great Depression. The "living tree" principle embodied in the Privy Council's ruling affected all subsequent debates about the BNA Act, but the judgment's recognition of full personhood for women, and their right to public office, had little impact. Until second-wave feminism emerged in the 1960s, Nellie's warning remained unfulfilled. Until 1968, out of 202 Senate appointments made by successive governments, only 9 (including Cairine Wilson's) were women. It was hardly a revolution.

CHAPTER NINE

Was It All Worth It?

Victoria, 1932–1951

> The idea of writing my own story has often come
> to me. . . . But when the urge came . . . it was
> driven out by the immediate present and its
> demands. It was not a compulsion, and running
> a house, raising five children, getting the vote for
> women, and baking the cake for the "talents tea"
> in the church were. But since I came to live in
> Victoria, British Columbia, I have thought of it
> more seriously. I have had more time to think. . . .
> The ladies' aid knows me no more; women have
> more rights than they are using.

During her years in Edmonton and Calgary, Nellie was frequently asked to address parent-teacher associations about
the need for women to participate in public life. She soon
learned what to expect—a crowd of women like her: "serious
minded, kind, motherly women, middle aged mostly church
women driven by a sense of duty." On one occasion, as she
strode off to deliver her usual remarks, she noticed a flurry of
"smartly dressed young women, mothers of one" skipping

out of their cars and into a hotel for a "tea dansant." Nellie gritted her teeth in exasperation. "They have not thought of joining a P.T.A. . . . It simply does not interest them." She visualized the "one child" returning home at four "to find an empty house, or a totally unconcerned maid, [and wandering] out into the street again to find his own pleasure."

Was Nellie just displaying starchy Methodist instincts, and her nineteenth-century upbringing, when she implied that women who weren't busily working to improve the lives of children and other women were traitors? Part of her irritation was that women who did not embrace their new opportunities were reinforcing traditional attitudes about female roles and abilities. At the same PTA meeting, she listened with horror as the male school principal directly contradicted her own message by remarking that women now belonged to so many organizations that homes were neglected—"late meals, milk bottles not set out at night, clocks not wound, salt-cellars not filled, slippers not warmed. . . ." She watched a wave of guilt sweep through the audience, as the women "wondered if after all they should have stayed home and made tidies for the living room chairs." She fumed that the fussy little principal never reproached the women who went dancing, "but any woman who attempts to improve any department of life is fair game for the critics."

At another level, however, Nellie's discomfort reflected the fact that Canada was changing almost too rapidly for her taste. The Canada of 1930 was vastly different from that of her Manitoba childhood. Since 1900, the population had almost doubled, and after 1918 ties with the mother country steadily loosened. Canadian lives were being shaped by forces unknown at her birth in 1873: cars, widely available electricity, the telephone. Main streets in towns like Manitou now boasted amenities unthinkable in her day— gas pumps, car dealerships, movie theatres. Agriculture and industry boomed because improved transportation allowed nationwide markets to emerge. In 1921, Canada had passed an important milestone: from then on, more people lived in cities than in rural areas. Department stores like Eaton's and Simpson's had expanded dramatically; corporate giants like Bell Canada and the Canada Cement Company monopolized their fields.

From Nellie's perspective, progress was measurable in the improvements to women's lives—and she didn't mean only access to political power and office. She welcomed the spread in Alberta and elsewhere of programs like mother's allowances, school nurses, travelling libraries, and the establishment of public schools where immigrant children could quickly acquire English. Nevertheless, she was exasperated by what she regarded as women's failure to live up to enfranchisement. The arrival of vacuum cleaners and washing machines had alleviated the drudgery of housework for those who could afford them. More women could now control their fertility through devices like rubber diaphragms. These advances were, for some women, at least as liberating as the vote. But Nellie, imbued from a young age with her mother's work ethic, couldn't accept how some women used their extra hours. "A great many women are wandering in a maze of discontent and disillusionment," she wrote. "Idle hands and empty minds make an explosive mixture. Having little to do, they do nothing; and doing nothing, they miss that sense of work well done which sustained their grandmothers." What was the point of all the effort made by Cora Hind, or Emily Murphy, or any of Nellie's fellow crusaders if women just wanted to dance?

In 1932, as Nellie McClung's sixtieth birthday approached, arthritis and incipient heart disease slowed her down. Wes's retirement was imminent, and all the children had now left home, so the McClungs decided to move to the West Coast. "We are saying goodbye," announced the Calgary *Albertan* on July 9, 1932, "to the kindly humorous, vigorous citizen who will leave behind a gap that cannot be filled." None of Nellie's friends in Alberta took at face value Nellie's insistence that she was going to retire from all her activities except writing. Their disbelief was well founded: as soon as the McClungs arrived in Victoria, Nellie was busy. The Women's Missionary Society "got after me, and I fell," a cheerful letter to a friend reads. "I spoke at two guest teas this week and will speak at one tomorrow. And I have two lectures to give. I think it is seven times I have addressed meetings, but I feel real well and am glad to be able to help a little."

Once Wes finally retired two years later, the McClungs decided to look for a house in the country, where Wes could pursue a dream he had always nurtured: a market garden. On a chilly, grey January day, when "no one could be enthusiastic about anything," they decided to visit Gordon Head, ten kilometres outside Victoria, to look at a small farm that had been empty for some months. As Wes drove the family Ford down a lane lined with cherry trees, the McClungs could see a dark green shingled bungalow, with a broken window and an unloved look. They left the car, walked round to the verandah at the front, and then, as Nellie recorded in the first essay in her volume *Leaves from Lantern Lane*, "The sun came out! A sudden, unexpected flood of light ran over the fields and down to the sea. It lingered on the bright red roof of a white house on the right, almost hidden in the trees; it caught the wings of a wind-mill on a water tower below us; . . . it glittered on a white sail out on the sea. And then it was gone and the woolly grayness rolled back. But we had seen the beauty of Gordon Head in that one bright, revealing flash."

After such a vision, Nellie was unstoppable. The McClungs moved into the bungalow as soon as the leaks were fixed. Since there were no street lights in the lane, they hung a ship's lantern above the garage and named the house "Lantern Lane." It would be Nellie's home until her death, sixteen years later. Wes planted his rows of beans, and Nellie, who had never really left her rural roots, made friends with all the neighbours. Walking home in the dark after a visit "made us think of the times we found our way home over Manitoba trails on moonless nights, with the wolves howling."

The tranquility of Lantern Lane went some way toward reconciling Nellie to a slower pace of life. She wrote a weekly column, syndicated in newspapers across Canada, that hums with the chin-up cheerfulness that she always adopted when she felt her age. She particularly enjoyed writing about the challenge of growing onions—a saga that lasted several years. But there was often an undercurrent of regret for goals unreached. "I am a woman with a past," she noted in one piece. "But when the fire burns, and I have the flower catalogue in my hands, I turn my back to the gray shades of disappointed hopes, and in imagination my soul goes forward."

Speaking invitations arrived from all over the country, and despite declining energy, she accepted several because she loved the adrenalin rush of performance. She had several stock speeches that aimed to inspire her listeners with hope: they had titles like "Romance in Everyday Life" and "The Adventure of Living." After the publication of *Clearing in the West*, the first volume of her autobiography, in 1935, she travelled as far as Ontario and Quebec to give readings. And the old crusading zeal could be sparked when she felt human rights were being compromised.

Soon after Nellie moved to Victoria, she had been caught up in the plight of Japanese Canadians, who faced relentless discrimination. They were denied the right to vote; excluded from most professions, the civil service, and teaching; and consistently forced to accept lower wages than Caucasian employees. Many of Nellie's friends, such as Emily Murphy, embraced the thoughtless racism that was endemic in Canada during this period. Pandering to white supremacist emotions, B.C. politicians had placed restrictions on the number of Japanese allowed to immigrate and the number of fishing licences granted. Nellie was outraged, and in 1935, she agreed to speak in a public debate at Vancouver's Empress Theatre on whether Japanese Canadians should be allowed to vote. "I could not take the responsibility of claiming for myself," she announced, "a privilege I wouldn't give to any-body else." The audience erupted with jeers and boos; the meeting's organizers looked around nervously, wondering whether missiles would start flying. But the plain-spoken, grey-haired woman on stage didn't flinch; instead, she just gripped the microphone more firmly. "In my opinion, every class and every creed of people should have equal rights. . . . I don't think the presence of well-mannered meditative Orientals would lower the tone of political meetings in Vancouver."

Hostility to Japanese Canadians, along with other immi-grant groups, including Doukhobors, mounted during the 1930s, but Nellie continued to urge that they all be treated with fairness. As war approached, Colonel George Drew, leader of the Ontario Conservative Party, demanded that the Japanese be deported. Nellie was outraged, noting that his opinion "must make the flesh of all decent people creep." Nellie's convictions did not waver, even after the Japanese bombed Pearl Harbor on December, 7, 1941. A month later, she wrote, "We have in this province of British Columbia 23,000 Japanese people, many of them natives of Canada and some of the second generation. We have an opportunity now of showing them that we do respect human rights and that democracy has a wide enough framework to give peace and security to all people of goodwill irrespective of race or colour. . . . We must not sink into Hitler's ways of persecution. We must not punish innocent people. The Canadian Japanese are not to blame for the treacherous attack on Pearl Harbor, nor for the other misdeeds of their misled people."

No articles by Nellie deploring the internment of Japanese Canadians have surfaced, and her biographers Mary Hallett and Marilyn Davis suggest that her editors may have asked her to avoid political matters. One of her newspaper columns begins, "Now don't be nervous, Mr Editor, I am not dealing with [conscription] in a political way." As the war progressed, she devoted many column inches to advising her readers on how to support the troops, and do more with less. However, she did write to the B.C. minister of education demanding that the government take responsibility for education in the internment camps.

Along with Senator Cairine Wilson (who was much more of an activist than Prime Minister King had anticipated) and MP Agnes Macphail, Nellie also worked hard to raise public awareness of what was happening to Jews in Nazi Germany. She lobbied Prime Minister King personally to at least admit Jewish children to Canada. She received only a noncommittal reply. In 1939, in a letter to Macphail, Nellie railed against public apathy: "The Refugee Problem is getting me down—I mean the Gov't's sit-tight attitude . . . We have to do something or be forever disgraced."

What most concerned Nellie McClung during these years, however, was the impact of the Great Depression, triggered by the crash of the New York stock market in 1929. By 1933, nearly one in five able-bodied men was unemployed, while women in the labour force were quietly forced into unwanted retirement. Annual incomes were halved, and as much as one-third of the nation faced destitution. Nellie no more had answers to the misery than did politicians in Ottawa, but she recognized the psychological as well as the physical suffering of the poor. There were too many unemployment experts, she wrote in one column, who did not understand the reality of unemployment: "Hunting for a job, going from place to place, getting the glassy eye from employers who point to the sign, 'No Help Required,' having doors slammed in their faces, sleeping where they can, eating at soup kitchens, or not eating at all—having that terrible, desolate feeling of not being wanted anywhere." When she spoke to audiences of comfortable middle-class women, she urged them to get involved in the provision and administration of welfare. "It is not enough that we give to unemployment relief or send vegetables to the Salvation Army." Those who had "little answers for big questions" (that the poor were always with us, or that the unemployed didn't really want to work) were complacent and ill-informed. Unlike many of those who shared these views, however, Nellie was not tempted to look to new political parties to find solutions to the problems. In 1932, her old ally from Winnipeg days, the Social Gospel leader J.S. Woodsworth, joined with various other labour and socialist groups to found a new socialist party, the Co-operative Commonwealth Federation (CCF). Woodsworth's aim was to develop in Canada "a distinctive type of Socialism." He wrote, "I refuse to follow slavishly the British model or the American model or the Russian model. We in Canada will solve our problems along our own lines."

Nellie did not believe that a "from the ground up" movement would work, and she remained loyal to the Liberals and the two-party system. "Individually, the CCF are excellent people," she announced, "though I resent their mousy air of superior virtue when they allude to the old parties. They seem to think . . . anyone who remains in either of the old parties is in the pay and service of the Big Interests." Much better, she thought, that progressive thinkers should join forces; otherwise they are "divided and subdivided, until their influence is watered down to nothing. You can chip down a good log, which might have been made into something beautiful and useful, until you have nothing but a pile of saw-dust!" Her own inclination was to revert to the kind of spiritual crusade that she had articulated in 1918. Once again, her rhetoric started to sound more like windy blather than a real plan of action: "We need . . . more people who have the vision of a new Canada. . . . We need new people, which is to say new hearts!"

The Conservative government of Richard Bennett, elected in 1930, had struggled to contain the worst aspects of the Depression with work camps and suppression of dissent. But Nellie's hero Mackenzie King was waiting in the wings to pick up the pieces, and she was elated when, with the slogan "King or Chaos," he won the 1935 election. The following year, he appointed Nellie McClung to the board of the newly reorganized Canadian Broadcasting Corporation—an institution that, in the coming years, would do much to bind Canada together. There had been privately owned radio stations in Canada since 1920, and by 1923, three Canadian households in four owned a radio. The new CBC was charged with the job of supervising radio stations and fostering a "national spirit."

The CBC appointment should have been a great pulpit for an outspoken woman who had already seen the potential of radio to reach remote rural communities. The only woman on the board, Nellie told a reporter that "women are the best listeners to radio" and lobbied hard to ensure that women's programs were about more than child rearing and recipes. In an article entitled "The Voice of Canada" she wrote, "Radio is the greatest university in the world, with the lowest fees, the largest student body and the easiest manner of entrance."

But Nellie found CBC board membership as frustrating as she had found being an opposition MLA during the 1920s. There is a photograph of the board members, sitting behind wooden tables that had been pulled into an angular U shape and piled high with papers. Most of the men, in their uniform of white shirts and striped ties, appear relaxed and confident. Nellie, sitting ramrod straight and wearing severe eyeglasses and an uncharacteristically stern expression, is squeezed into a corner seat and is clearly uncomfortable. Somehow, her concerns always got submerged. Board meetings were held only two or three times a year, so it was hard to remain connected to the enterprise. Only one of the other governors was a fellow westerner, and CBC stations in Toronto and Montreal were always given priority. Nellie's campaigns to get more women on air were sabotaged by prejudice. Women's voices were said to be too high pitched for transmission. A Niagara Falls newspaper scoffed, "We'd like to hear one of them handle a professional hockey game this winter."

Most depressing for a temperance advocate was the proposal that liquor advertising should be allowed on the airwaves. Once again, Nellie's sense of humour and sunny personality disappeared when arguing this issue. The discussions were so rancorous that even Prime Minister King got involved as Nellie challenged Leonard Brockington, chairman of the board, whom she suspected of being pro–liquor ads. Nellie never forgave herself for another nasty incident during this dispute, when a Jewish opponent on the board disagreed with her. As a general principle, as she recorded in her memoirs, she regarded anti-Semitism as "a sure sign of moral decay." But on this occasion, as she later confessed to her son Mark, "I was so annoyed with him that I said . . . 'Mr. So-and-so, you're the sort of Jew that almost makes me an anti-Semite.'" As soon as she had spoken, she could have bitten her tongue: she quickly grabbed her opponent's hand and apologized profusely. Describing the incident to Mark, she had tears in her eyes: "To say such a thing, to another human being—just intolerable."

In retrospect, Nellie's appointment to the CBC board looks like a token gesture to Canadian women. King gave her another token appointment in 1938, when he invited her to serve as a Canadian delegate to that year's session of the League of Nations in Geneva. Charlotte Whitton, the mayor of Ottawa who had previously been a delegate to Geneva, warned Nellie that she would be "sickeningly disillusioned with the speeches in the Assembly." Nevertheless, as Nellie packed her suits and a splendid new evening dress into her trunk and kissed Wes goodbye, her enthusiasm remained undented.

Sailing on the *Empress of Britain* from Quebec, Nellie arrived in France on September 1, 1938, where she met her son Mark, who was a Rhodes Scholar at Oxford University. Once they reached Geneva, however, her spirits sagged. In theory, the forty-seven-member League embodied so much of what she believed in: international harmony achieved through co-operation and conciliation, and concern for the underprivileged. In practice, she watched the session begin "in a spirit of fear and distrust, regret and recrimination." She had been assigned to the Fifth Committee dealing with social issues such as refugees and control of narcotics. The committee was soon bogged down in process, which Nellie found excruciating: "Arguments would run on for half an hour at a time about trivialities. One day I made bold to tell them that I thought if nobody cared who got the credit, much more could be accomplished, and for this I was reprimanded, privately, by one member of the Canadian contingent."

Meanwhile, Hitler was declaring his intention to invade Czechoslovakia. Delegates crouched around radios to listen to the German führer's shrill, menacing demagoguery, while the speeches at Nellie's committee began to sound like "conversations at a funeral," as members rushed home. Nellie was relieved when she and Mark finally left for Paris, where they heard about the Munich Agreement between Britain, France, and Germany. When she reflected in the second volume of her memoirs, *The Stream Runs Fast*, on her experience at the League, she insisted she didn't regret seeing "that gleaming white palace, built by many nations." But she described it as a mansion with every technological gizmo imaginable, lacking only one thing—electricity. "The sterility of the League smote my heart with a sense of helplessness."

By the time war broke out in Europe in 1939, Nellie McClung was safely back in Victoria. The following year, the sixty-seven-year-old who had seemed so indefatigable had a heart attack while attending a CBC board meeting in Ottawa. Her doctor instructed her firmly to scale back. Nellie hid her disappointment in a flurry of flippancy. "I'm washed up and finished! I can no longer drive a car, work in the garden or travel, must avoid crowds, eat sparingly, observe one general rule: 'If you like it, avoid it!'" But she could still sit at her desk and write. Many of her columns between 1939 and 1945 dealt with the roles women were taking in the war effort. The old campaigner raged against the way women continued to have second-class status, despite the legal rights she had helped them achieve. She lobbied for women to take charge of food distribution for the army, because she felt that they had superior knowledge of nutrition and household management. When women were accepted into the Canadian Forces, she protested vigorously that they were not paid on the same scale as men. Women "were declared persons in 1929," she wrote, "but now they are rated in comparison with men as nine to thirteen."

One day her son Mark, splendid in his new naval uniform, arrived to visit his elderly mother. They greeted each other warmly, and he sat down expecting a few gentle enquiries about his plans. Instead, he found himself blushing as his mother interrogated him as to whether naval women received the same information on contraception as men got. After the war, Nellie was infuriated by the widespread assumption that women should abandon jobs in shops and offices and make way for returning soldiers. "The insulting part of it," she noted in a *Victoria Times* column, "is this loathsome idea that women would like it."

In 1944, the McClungs suffered a shattering blow. Their eldest son, a successful prosecuting attorney for the Alberta department of justice, killed himself. Jack McClung had somehow become involved in a minor fraud, and had shot himself in remorse. Alcohol had played a role, although his mother felt the root cause of her son's action lay in the psychological wounds sustained in the trenches of the First World War. Both Wes and Nellie were devastated by Jack's death: Nellie wrote that she now understood "why people stop the clock and draw the blinds" when faced with such loss. Only her strong faith, and the support of family and friends, helped her surmount the loss. She silently returned to her writing desk, stared out of the window at the arbutus tree in the middle of her neighbour's field, and took up her pen again. *The Stream Runs Fast*, which takes her story from her marriage to Wes in 1896 to her years as an "old craft, riding at anchor in a safe harbor," was published in 1945. The following year, on August 25, 1946, the McClungs celebrated their golden wedding anniversary. So much for McClung critics who had whispered that feminism is a sure marriage wrecker.

A lively picture of the McClung household during these years appeared in the *Canadian Home Journal* in October 1947. The Toronto writer Margaret Ecker Francis travelled across the country to pay homage to "the grey-haired novelist, who will be seventy-four on 20 October." Francis expected to talk to a gentle old soul wallowing in nostalgia; instead, she encountered a firebrand still looking for action. "She didn't look her years. She didn't talk her years." Nellie described to Francis her intention of publishing another novel, then launched into a discussion of a recent CBC broadcast by correspondent Matthew Halton. "It was obvious," wrote the startled young journalist, "that Lantern Lane is no quiet cloister, aloof from the world, but rather a radio set tuned to sound waves of affairs and opinions."

Francis's article also caught the character of the man who had always been at Nellie's side, giving her the secure family base from which she could launch her campaigns. "A tall, slightly-stooped man, with unruly hair and a twinkle in his eye, hesitated for a moment at the door," wrote Francis. She went on to describe how Wes put a protective hand on his wife's arm and warned her not to overtax herself. The elderly couple exchanged smiles "full of youthfulness and of some private joke. Together, somehow, they seemed much younger than they did separately." Wes McClung told Francis that he was "both model and critic when my wife needs either."

Despite the brave front, Nellie's health was failing. She struggled to keep up her voluminous correspondence, but the list of activities that were beyond her steadily lengthened. Soon she could not attend church, or walk down to the beach, or receive too many guests.

Another visitor was a fellow member of the Canadian Authors Association. He found Nellie sitting quietly in her garden, and remarked on the serenity of the scene. Nellie gave a wry smile. "If I were only a few years younger," she said, "I'd move tomorrow to Winnipeg with its blizzards." Had it all been worth it? If Nellie McClung had been asked this question, she would have given a vigorous nod. But, as she said in her memoirs, "still I cannot look back without regret. I can see too many places where I could have been more obedient to the heavenly vision . . . of a better world."

As the days shortened at the end of the summer of 1951, Wes McClung watched his wife slip away. On one occasion, he found her lying motionless, and thought the end had come. But then she opened her eyes, smiled at him, and before she closed them again, said, "Oh, I'm still here! I'll never believe I'm dead till I see it in the paper." Nellie remained astringent until the end. "I have a few questions I will ask if happily I arrive at the heavenly country. . . . Especially do I want to know how it is that a just God has allowed the sins of the fathers to be visited on the children. Even the virtues of the mothers, inherited by the same law, do not balance the account." Nellie McClung died in her bed at Lantern Lane on September 1, 1951, aged seventy-nine. Five years later, Wes joined her in the Victoria cemetery. Both

McClungs remained secure in their deep Christian faith until the end. As Nellie had written in 1917, "When the black curtain of death falls on life's troubled scenes, there will appear on it these words in letters of gold, 'End of Part I. Part II will follow immediately.'"

CHAPTER TEN

How Did Nellie Change Canada?

> I have seen my country emerge from obscurity into one of the truly great nations of the world. I have seen strange things come to pass in the short span of one lifetime, and I hasten to set it down while the light holds. People must know the past to understand the present and face the future.

Most Canadian newspapers carried obituaries of Nellie McClung. But they were brief, and many focused on her sixteen books and conventional family life rather than her achievements as an early feminist. In an editorial three days after her death, the *Globe and Mail* noted that "her life was extraordinary in many ways, especially as she found time for the normal duties of wife and mother in the midst of her other interests." (The editorialist also observed that "unlike so many who allow a great enthusiasm for life free rein, she achieved much.") The *Toronto Daily Star* devoted only half a paragraph to her political achievements, before going on to describe her as "a womanly woman who had a happy family life and was devoted to her children. She might appropriately be remembered as Mrs. Western Canada."

It was as though Canadians, by 1951, didn't really want to remember all those prewar battles for women's right to vote, or to sit in the Senate, or to preach in the United Church, or to stand shoulder to shoulder with men in the armed forces or on the factory floor. The country was in the first flush of postwar prosperity: suburbs were starting to sprawl over farmland, and yellow school buses trundled along country roads. In the smudgy photo that accompanied some of those obituaries, Nellie's wire-framed glasses and direct gaze were disconcertingly severe. Far more exciting were other items in those same newspapers—articles about glittering company headquarters in downtown Toronto, or advertisements for new face creams, kitchen appliances, and Oldsmobiles. The woman celebrated in popular culture was a gingham-aproned domestic diva devoted to the interests of home, husband, and offspring.

For a few years, Nellie McClung seemed to be sliding into the shadows of the past. However, that wasn't the last of Nellie. As the Women's Movement blossomed in the 1960s, academics and writers rediscovered the first wave of feminists of the late nineteenth and early twentieth century who had demanded equality and justice. There were many early activists to celebrate: Emily Stowe, the first woman to practise medicine in Canada and a prominent Toronto suffrage campaigner; Adelaide Hoodless, who spawned a worldwide organization when she founded the first Women's Institute in 1897; Clara Brett Martin, the first woman admitted to the Ontario bar in 1897; and all Nellie's allies from Winnipeg and Alberta.

Yet Nellie McClung has pulled ahead of this redoubtable sisterhood in the battle for public recognition. By the end of the twentieth century, when Canadians were polled for the most important woman in their history, Nellie's name was the one most often mentioned (if, that is, any name was mentioned: in the majority of interviews, the pollster was met with a blank stare). Why?

Nellie had the advantage of being a woman who straddled Canada from east to west in the nation-building phase of our history. Born in Ontario, she was politically active in Manitoba, Alberta, and British Columbia, and her books were read coast to coast. The wit that won her a following in her own day also resonated with the later, Betty Friedan generation. "If you're going to quote anybody," says Veronica Strong-Boag, professor of women's studies at the University of British Columbia, "you want to quote Nellie. She was the mistress of the one-liner." How could the Bronfman Foundation (now Historica) resist making her historic encounter with Premier Roblin in 1914 one of the first productions in their Heritage Minutes series?

At the same time, there was so much more to Nellie than a quick tongue. Her wit, and the motherly air celebrated in her obituaries, put a human face on challenging ideas. She used her skill as a platform speaker to win audiences over rather than antagonize them. She liked most people, and they liked her, which meant that they didn't find her or her ideas so threatening. She spoke in a tone that her listeners found both familiar and comfortable—the soft western accent of the early pioneers, and the rolling cadences of the pulpit. Her humble origins, no-nonsense lack of pretension, and strong sense of justice fostered a universal appeal. Her priority was not the predicament of educated women who wanted to enter professions, but the plight of farmers' wives and factory workers, and the vulnerability of immigrants struggling to adapt to an alien culture. So she was able quietly to nudge people in the direction that she wanted them to go. "She made people laugh," points out Strong-Boag, "and at the same time she made them think seriously about the feminist enterprise." The violent tactics of British suffragettes like Emmeline and Sylvia Pankhurst, and the aggressive rhetoric of America's Elizabeth Cady Stanton and Susan B. Anthony, were not Nellie's style. Nor was the tendency within the British and American suffrage movements to reflect exclusively the frustrations of middle-class women.

This inclusiveness was her major contribution to the history of feminism in Canada, and it is what sustains her reputation as the pivotal woman activist of her day. Her pragmatism and her personal appeal kept Canadian feminism firmly in the political mainstream rather than marginalized on the left. Although her ideas were radical, she herself was no revolutionary, preferring to stay safely within the Liberal tent. She sympathized with many of the goals of her friends in the Social Gospel movement and the CCF (the predecessor of today's New Democratic Party), but that was not enough to persuade her to support movements with little hope of achieving political power. "She stayed in the Liberal centre," points out Strong-Boag, "and her acceptance there helped shape Canadian feminism right through to the 1980s. That's how Canadians got the 1967 Royal Commission on the Status of Women. No other English-speaking country incorporated feminism into the establishment."

When I began to explore Nellie's life, I was frustrated by how little material I could lay my hands on. When she herself sat down to write the second volume of her memoirs, she drew on diaries that she had kept since 1912, and scrapbooks of newspaper clippings. But her daughter, Florence, burned those diaries and personal papers—whether at Nellie's request, or on her own initiative, I don't know. This makes the private Nellie hard to locate. I could only speculate about the compromises she had to make, or her feelings when she was (as mentioned briefly in *The Stream Runs Fast*) being "accused, attacked and maligned [and] . . . burned in effigy." Although she lived well into the age of film, I could find no black-and-white footage of Nellie making her audience roar with laughter and her enemies seethe with frustration. There are her own published memoirs, and the many sharp quips and quotations, but they present the public Nellie.

I finally found one direct connection to Nellie McClung. If you go to http://archives.cbc.ca and enter "Nellie McClung" into the search box, you can hear a brief clip of Nellie speaking in 1938, at the ceremony celebrating the Persons Case in the Senate foyer. You can catch the trace of a Dundee burr inherited from her mother, the sharp intelligence, the cadence of a prairie preacher, and the barely suppressed amusement as she intersperses serious remarks with impish humour. For me, the sound of her voice conjured up the woman and her whole story, from the prairie childhood to the fearless and deeply religious fighter.

Nellie herself was unfailingly modest about her achievements—she was too busy trying to get things done to spend
her energy on claiming credit. As she would be the first to
point out, any success was the result of the collective efforts
of colleagues and allies. This is why the Famous Five statue
on Parliament Hill is a fitting memorial to early feminists.
All the other statues on the Hill depict their subjects as lon-
ers on pedestals (or, in Queen Elizabeth II's case, on a horse
and a pedestal). Nellie McClung is depicted by sculptor
Barbara Paterson alongside her four fellow petitioners from
the 1929 Persons Case: Emily Murphy, Irene Parlby, Louise
McKinney, and Henrietta Muir Edwards. The statues sup-
posedly catch the moment when the five women have heard
that the Privy Council Office in London has declared that
women are persons. The Famous Five stand or sit at ground
level, radiating a kind of group warmth, and inviting tourists
to approach or even join them by sitting on a vacant chair.
Four of the five display the dignity and self-restraint expected of women of their period, but one of the bronze figures
exuberantly waves a piece of paper on which the judicial
decision is printed in large letters (and—a nice anachro-
nism—in both official languages). The woman caught in
this spontaneous gesture—the woman sporting a natty
cloche hat and a gleeful smile—is, of course, Nellie.

1830   John Mooney, aged eighteen, arrives in
      Canada from Ireland.

1858   John Mooney marries Letitia McCurdy, a
      Scottish immigrant twenty years younger than
      him.

1859   William Mooney is born on the Mooney farm
      on Garafraxa Road, 1.5 kilometres south of
      Chatsworth, in Grey County, Canada West
      (Ontario).

1861   George Mooney is born.

1867   Elizabeth (Lizzie) is born. Under the British
      North America Act, the Canadian
      Confederation unites Ontario, Quebec, Nova
      Scotia, and New Brunswick.

1868   Jack Mooney is born.

1869–70 Louis Riel leads the Red River Rebellion and
      orders the execution of Thomas Scott, an
      Ontario Orangeman. He then flees to the
      United States. The federal government in

Ottawa creates Manitoba, and opens the new province up for settlement.

1871   Hannah Mooney is born.

1873   Nellie Letitia Mooney is born.

1874   The first Canadian branch of the Women's Christian Temperance Union (WCTU) is established in Ontario.

1876   Dr. Emily Stowe, the first woman to practise medicine in Canada, founds Canada's first suffrage group, the Toronto Women's Literary Club.

1880   The Mooney family moves west, and settles on the prairie near the Souris River, southeast of Brandon, in southern Manitoba.

1883   Frank Schultz is appointed teacher in the newly built Northfield School, three kilometres from the Mooney farm. Nellie learns to read.

1885   The Northwest Rebellion triggers clashes between Métis and government troops (the North West Mounted Police, Canadian militia, and some British soldiers). The Battle

of Batoche, in southern Saskatchewan, leads
to the surrender of Louis Riel on May 15,
and the collapse of Métis resistance to
Ottawa's authority. Louis Riel is hanged
on November 7.

1889	Nellie moves to Winnipeg to attend the normal school and train as a teacher.
1890	Nellie takes up her first teaching position at Hazel School, near Manitou.
1892	Nellie boards with the McClung family in Manitou, where she joins the WCTU, starts writing, and meets her future husband.
1896	Nellie marries Wes McClung.
1897	John Wesley (Jack) McClung is born.
1899	Florence McClung is born.
1900	Paul McClung is born. In the United States, women in the states of Wyoming, Utah, Colorado, and Idaho get the vote. New Zealand becomes the first country to grant women suffrage.

1903   The Canadian Women's Press Club is formed. In Britain, Emmeline Pankhurst founds the National Women's Social and Political Union.

1906   Horace McClung is born.

1907   Nellie gives her first public speech at a WCTU convention in Manitou.

1908   *Sowing Seeds in Danny* is published and becomes a bestseller.

1910   *The Second Chance*, the second in Nellie's Pearlie Watson trilogy, is published.

1911   The McClungs move to Winnipeg and their fifth child, Mark, is born.

1912   Nellie and fourteen other Winnipeg women found the Political Equality League, and Nellie makes women's suffrage her main focus.

1913   In England, Emmeline Pankhurst is imprisoned for inciting suffragettes to use explosives.

1914   Nellie, posing as Premier Rodmond Roblin, is the star of the Political Equality League's mock parliament. Despite the league's best efforts,

Roblin's Conservative government is re-elected.
Britain declares war on Germany, and Canada
automatically follows Britain's lead. In
December, the McClungs move to Edmonton.

1915   Nellie joins the Edmonton Equal Franchise
        League, meets Emily Murphy and Alice
        Jamieson, and publishes *In Times Like These*.
        Prohibition is introduced in Alberta. Jack
        McClung enlists.

1916   Women receive the right to vote in Manitoba,
        Saskatchewan, and Alberta. Nellie embarks on
        a six-week, forty-city tour of the United
        States, accompanied by her daughter,
        Florence.

1918   Nellie attends the Women's War Conference
        in Ottawa in February. In November, the
        First World War ends. Women get the right
        to vote in federal elections.

1919   The General Strike shuts down Winnipeg for
        five weeks; ten strike leaders, including J.S.
        Woodsworth, are arrested.

1920   Women in the United States get the right to
        vote in federal elections.

1921	Nellie travels to England as a delegate to the Fifth Ecumenical Methodist Conference, and calls for the ordination of women. She is elected as a Liberal MLA to the Alberta legislature.
1923	The McClung family moves to Calgary. Alberta relaxes its liquor legislation.
1924	Alberta and Saskatchewan legislate the sale of alcoholic beverages under government control.
1925	The United Church is established.
1926	Nellie is defeated in the Alberta election.
1927	Emily Murphy invites Nellie, Henrietta Muir Edwards, Louise McKinney, and Irene Parlby to join her in petitioning the Supreme Court regarding the definition of "persons."
1928	The Supreme Court decides that, under the BNA Act, women are not "persons."
1929	The Judicial Committee of the Privy Council reverses this decision, and declares that women are persons. On October 24, the U.S. stock exchange collapses, triggering the Great Depression.

1930	Cairine Wilson is appointed to the Canadian Senate.
1932	Wes and Nellie McClung move to Victoria. J.S. Woodsworth co-founds a new political party, the Co-operative Commonwealth Federation (CCF).
1935	The McClungs buy their last home in Gordon Head, ten kilometres outside Victoria, and name it "Lantern Lane." *Clearing in the West*, the first volume of Nellie's memoirs, is published.
1936	Nellie is appointed to the CBC's first Board of Broadcast Governors. The United Church finally accepts the ordination of women.
1938	Nellie travels to Geneva as part of the Canadian delegation to the League of Nations. Hitler invades Austria.
1939	Britain declares war on Germany; Canada follows suit a few days later.
1940	Nellie suffers a heart attack and resigns from the CBC board.
1944	Jack McClung commits suicide in Edmonton.

1945   Germany surrenders to the Allies.
The Stream Runs Fast, the second volume
of Nellie's memoirs, is published.

1946   Wes and Nellie McClung celebrate their
fiftieth wedding anniversary.

1951   Nellie McClung dies in Victoria and is buried
at the Royal Oak Burial Park, Saanich, British
Columbia.

SOURCES

Because Florence McClung burnt many of her mother's letters, journals, scrapbooks, and collection of newspaper clippings, there is a dearth of primary materials for Nellie McClung. Most of her papers are held at the British Columbia Provincial Archives in Victoria; Library and Archives Canada, in Ottawa, also has materials relating to her, her son Mark McClung, and Eula Lapp. In addition, there are her sixteen published books: of these, the Pearlie Watson trilogy (*Sowing Seeds in Danny, The Second Chance,* and *Purple Springs*) is the most fun to read, and *In Times Like These* is the most revealing about McClung's politics and personality.

Candace Savage's anthology, *Our Nell: A Scrapbook Biography of Nellie L. McClung* (Saskatoon: Western Producer Prairie Books, 1979), provided me with many direct quotations from McClung. I also drew on magazine articles by and about McClung, including the following:

Francis, Margaret Ecker. "Nellie McClung," *Canadian Home Journal,* October 1947.

McClung, Nellie L. "Can a Woman Raise a Family and Have a Career?" *Maclean's,* February 1928.

McClung, Nellie L. "A Woman on the Warpath," *Maclean's,* January 1920.

Symmes, Natalie. "Nellie McClung of the West," *Canada Monthly,* February 1916.

Most previous biographies of McClung have been written for young adults; one of the best is Margaret MacPherson's *Nellie McClung: Voice for the Voiceless* (Montreal: XYZ Publishing, 2003). I also read several earlier biographies of McClung:

Hallett, Mary, and Marilyn Davis. *Firing the Heather: The Life and Times of Nellie McClung* (Calgary: Fifth House, 1994).

Hancock, Carol L. *No Small Legacy* (Winfield, BC: Wood Lake Books, 1986).

For background on McClung's era, I referred to the following books:

Blanchard, Jim. *Winnipeg 1912* (Winnipeg: University of Manitoba Press, 2005).

Gray, James. *Booze: When Whiskey Ruled the West* (Calgary: Fifth House, 1995).

———. *The Winter Years: The Depression on the Prairies* (Calgary: Fifth House, 2003).

Morton, W.L. *Manitoba: A History*, 2nd ed. (Toronto: University of Toronto Press, 1976).

For information on the early suffrage movement and the Persons Case, I read the following books and articles:

Atkinson, Diane. *The Purple, White & Green: Suffragettes in London, 1906–1914* (London: Museum of London, 1992).

Bacchi, Carol Lee. *Liberation Deferred? The Ideas of the English Canadian Suffragists, 1877–1918* (Toronto: University of Toronto Press, 1982).

Betcherman, Lita-Rose. *Ernest Lapointe: Mackenzie King's Great Quebec Lieutenant* (Toronto: University of Toronto Press, 2002).

Cleverdon, Catherine L. *The Woman Suffrage Movement in Canada* (Toronto: University of Toronto Press, 1950; reprint, 1974).

Hacker, Carlotta. *E. Cora Hind* (Don Mills, ON: Fitzhenry and Whiteside, 1979).

Mitchell, David. *Queen Christina: A Biography of Christabel Pankhurst* (London: Macdonald and Jane's, 1977).

Sanders, Byrne Hope. *Famous Women: Carr, Hind, Gullen, Murphy* (Toronto: Clarke, Irwin, 1958).

Sharpe, Robert J., and Patricia I. McMahon. *The Persons Case: The Origins and Legacy of the Fight for Legal Personhood* (Toronto: University of Toronto Press, 2007).

Strong-Boag, Veronica. "'Ever a Crusader': Nellie McClung, First Wave Feminist" in Veronica Strong-Boag and Anita Clair Fellman, eds., *Rethinking Canada: The Promise of Women's History*, 2nd ed. (Toronto: Copp Clark Pitman, 1991).

For discussions on McClung's achievements, I turned to the following:

Davis, Marilyn, ed. Introduction to *Stories Subversive: Through the Field with Gloves Off: Short Fiction by Nellie L. McClung* (Ottawa: University of Ottawa Press, 1996).

Devereux, Cecily. *Growing a Race: Nellie L. McClung and the Fiction of Eugenic Feminism* (Montreal and Kingston: McGill-Queen's University Press, 2005).

Fiamengo, Janice. "Rediscovering Our Foremothers Again: Racial Ideas of Canada's Early Feminists, 1885–1945" in Mona Gleason and Adele Perry, eds., *Rethinking Canada: The Promise of Women's History*, 5th ed. (Don Mills, ON: Oxford University Press, 2006).

Karr, Clarence. *Authors and Audiences: Popular Canadian Fiction in the Early Twentieth Century* (Montreal and Kingston: McGill-Queen's University Press, 2000).

Strong-Boag, Veronica, and Michelle Lynn Rosa. Introduction to *Nellie McClung: The Complete Autobiography* (Peterborough, ON: Broadview Press, 2003).

The accusation of plagiarism is contained in the 2007 book *Over Canadian Trails*, edited by Klaus Martens and published in Germany by Köenigshausen & Neumann. I am grateful to Bill Redekop at the *Winnipeg Free Press* for drawing it to my attention.

ACKNOWLEDGMENTS

Marcia McClung, Nellie McClung's granddaughter, has been a source of encouragement and information through-out the writing process, and I am in her debt. Darlene Wallcraft, at Manitoba's Archibald Historical Museum, west of Manitou, kindly showed me two buildings associated with Nellie McClung (including the house where the McClungs lived between 1904 and 1911) that have been relocated to the museum. I am also grateful for the insights, intellectual rigour, and reading suggestions provided by Dr. Veronica Strong-Boag of the University of British Columbia, Dr. Michael Peterman of Trent University, and Dr. Duncan McDowall and Dr. Sandy Campbell, both of Carleton University. I am particularly grateful to Sandy for providing me with the quote in Chapter 8 from Nellie's let-ter to Lorne Pierce, taken from the Pierce papers at Queen's University archives, and to Hon. Mr. Justice Robert Sharpe, of the Ontario Court of Appeal, for allowing me to see the proofs of the book he co-authored with Patricia McMahon, *The Persons Case: The Origins and Legacy of the Fight for Legal Personhood.* The staff at Library and Archives Canada were, as usual, extremely helpful: Rosemary Bergeron, archivist for film and broadcasting in LAC's Special Collections Branch, located for me the sole recording of Nellie's voice that I have found. Thanks to Ernest Hillen, Marta Tomins, Richard Gwyn, Sheila Williams, and Patricia Potts for reading parts or all of the manuscript and giving great feedback. And thanks to Wendy Bryans, Maureen Boyd, Judith Moses, and Cathy Beehan for exploring the Canadian stereotype with me.

Most important, I would like to thank John Ralston Saul for inviting me to contribute to the series Extraordinary Canadians, for giving great editorial feedback, and for alerting me to the role played by Ernest Lapointe in the Persons Case. I am grateful to Diane Turbide and Tracy Bordian at Penguin Group (Canada), copy editor Marcia Gallego, and my agent, John Pearce. And as usual, I owe my husband, George Anderson, big time.

— COLLECT THEM ALL —

René Lévesque
by DANIEL POLIQUIN

Nellie McClung
by CHARLOTTE GRAY

Marshall McLuhan
by DOUGLAS COUPLAND

L.M. Montgomery
by JANE URQUHART

Lester B. Pearson
by ANDREW COHEN

Maurice Richard
by CHARLES FORAN

Mordecai Richler
by M.G. VASSANJI

Louis Riel &
Gabriel Dumont
by JOSEPH BOYDEN

Pierre Elliott Trudeau
by NINO RICCI

EXTRAORDINARY
CANADIANS

Why They Mattered Then.
Why They Matter Now.